C000000153

PRAISE FOR

ARCHBISHOP BENSON'S HUMMING TOP
& OTHER REFLECTIONS

Archbishop Benson's Humming Top propels us from Greek hats to gardens, via compassion fatigue and hunting parsons to the songbirds of Istanbul. Underpinning and uniting these wide-ranging reflections is the conviction that God is to be found in stillness and silence, and that we need to be able to listen if we are to hear the still, small voice.

Adrian Leak has created a box of delights: quirky and thoughtful, with plenty of still centres, to be dipped into and savoured: nourishment for the soul, with no damage to the waistline.

CAROLINE CHARTRES
Features Editor, Church Times

There is always grace, eloquence and wisdom in Adrian Leak's writing. He offers reflections on simple, familiar matters with poetic richness. Common sense, such as Adrian has in abundance, is as rare as it is valuable.

It has been said "As the tribe is dying, the dance gets faster". Adrian shows a different way: how by paying respect to others, we grow in confidence; how humility is a step on the path to resilience. These characteristics are needed (as much as they are under-valued) in the Church today. This is a book of gentle, honest and grace-filled hope.

ROBERT COTTON
Rector of Holy Trinity, Guildford,
Honorary Canon of Guildford Cathedral.

To Jilly & Arian

ARCHBISHOP BENSON'S
HUMMING TOP

& OTHER REFLECTIONS

with best wishes

Arian Leak xi/2018

ADRIAN LEAK

The Book Guild Ltd

First published in Great Britain in 2018 by
The Book Guild Ltd
9 Priory Business Park
Wistow Road, Kibworth
Leicestershire, LE8 0RX
Freephone: 0800 999 2982
www.bookguild.co.uk
Email: info@bookguild.co.uk
Twitter: @bookguild

Typeset in Aldine401 BT

Printed and bound in Great Britain by CPI Group (UK) Ltd, Croydon, CR0 4YY

ISBN 978 1912575 220

British Library Cataloguing in Publication Data.
A catalogue record for this book is available from the British Library.

To Daniel, Laura, Chloë and Alexander
with love

CONTENTS

FOREWORD

by Anthony Russell

Everyone who writes knows that it is easier to produce a lengthy book than a short piece, which is both interesting and amusing. Many parish priests find this one of the most demanding aspects of their role, for they are required to produce 'just a few words' for a wide variety of occasions in addition to one (or several) sermons per week.

In Adrian Leak's writing, one immediately feels one is in the hands of someone who can be trusted and has a gift for the constant and demanding role of writing such pieces with great frequency. He has already proved in his first volume, *Nebuchadnezzar's Marmalade Pot*, that, as the psalmist says, he 'has the pen of a ready writer'.

This collection of articles and sermons follows the path which he has already established as his own, and includes observations on the rural community, extracts from sermons for special occasions, articles and historical reflections. There are few books in which Archbishop Benson, Omar Khayyam and the faithful ministry of the Curé d'Ars receive a mention within neighbouring paragraphs.

He is able to keep the reader in touch with the changes in the church's year and the seasons. He finds material everywhere, in the hymn book and in the history of the church. He even finds room for an accessible explanation of the mysteries of the Trinity. George Herbert receives many mentions.

A Bishop writes, in reviewing the earlier volume, 'Letters from the clergy in parish magazines can be dreadfully dull'.

There is nothing dull about this compilation of observations and reflections. Fortunate is the parish that has a priest with such a well-stocked mind and the ability to weave such material into his parish newsletters and sermons.

+ Anthony

(Anthony Russell is a former Bishop of Ely, and author of *The Country Parson*)

ARCHBISHOP BENSON'S HUMMING TOP

(From a sermon preached at the Sung Eucharist in York Minster on the second Sunday in Lent 1983, it being the 350th anniversary of the death of George Herbert)

When Archibald Campbell Tait was appointed to the vacant see of London in 1856, he received from Benjamin Jowett, master of Balliol, the following message: 'The only advice I should venture to offer is that you should do as little as possible.'

Sadly for the diocese of London, and sadly for the man himself, Tait ignored those wise words. Seizing the reins of episcopal office he drove himself, his diocese, and, later, when he became the Archbishop of Canterbury, he drove the entire Church of England into a frenzy of activity.

In his obsession he was not alone. His successor to the Chair of St Augustine, Edward White Benson, described his own life as a bishop in words that must ever haunt the Church of England:

> *You have no idea what life is becoming to me. A humming top is the only thing that resembles it: perpetual motion, very dizzy, hollow within, keeping up a continual buzz.*

That was over one hundred and fifty years ago. The Church has not changed. The immense abilities and tireless energy of those great Victorian bishops – men like Blomfield of London, Wilberforce of Oxford and Thomson of York – stamped upon the modern Church the impress of ceaseless activity. The Church Militant became the Church Active, the Church Active became the Church Busy, and the Church

Busy runs the risk today of becoming the Church Busybody. E M Forster's words, 'Poor talkative little Christianity', are uncomfortably true.

The compulsion to do things grips us clergy in its vice. From the most junior assistant curate to the most senior incumbent, from the greenest team vicar to the ripest archdeacon, from the latest ordinand to the Primate of All England himself, we are obsessed with the need to do things.

Like Benson's humming top, we spin in tight gyrations. Equipped with our action packs, sustained by our resource kits, encumbered by our reports, trammelled by our working parties (those modern chimeras whose proceedings are no party and whose conclusions seldom work) and driven by a fear of failure, we stagger from commission to committee, from board to panel, and from synod to council. And to what end? For what reason do we go a-whoring after our own inventions?

Isaiah prophesied to his people: 'Thus says the Lord, the Holy One of Israel, "In returning and rest ye shall be saved; in quietness and confidence shall be your strength: and ye would not."'

St Jean Vianney (1786–1850), known as the *Curé d'Ars,* was the parish priest of a tiny village in rural France. Apart from the duties of a priest – he said his prayers, administered the sacraments, preached, catechised, visited the sick – he did very little that would now be recognised in the Church of England as evidence of an active and outgoing ministry. He attended no courses, he organised no missions, he sat on no committees, he answered no questionnaires, he read no diocesan reports, he set no targets and he designed no forward programmes. And yet, the world came to his church to hear his words, which were full of grace, and to receive his counsel, which was full of wisdom.

One day he noticed a peasant sitting in church, silently

looking at the tabernacle in which the Blessed Sacrament was reserved. When the *curé* asked what he was doing, the peasant replied, 'I look at him and he looks at me.'

The 'prayer of simple regard', a silent stillness in the presence of our Lord, is hard to achieve in an overactive life, but it is one to which all of us must aim. Words and lists, petitions and intercessions, that much overused form of prayer, can be just busy distractions from the silent prayer of simple regard. Just as initiatives, programmes, targets and action plans can be no more than symptoms of panic in a church that seems to have lost its faith.

'In returning and rest ye shall be saved; in quietness and confidence shall be your strength.' Those words were first uttered in ancient Israel by Isaiah in his sermon to an anxious and faithless people. They are true for our Church today.

THE DAY LIES OPEN BEFORE US

Awake! For Morning in the Bowl of Night
Has flung the Stone that puts the Stars to Flight:
And Lo! The Hunter of the East has caught
The Sultan's Turret in a Noose of Light.

Edward Fitzgerald (1809–1883)
Omar Khayyam (1048–1131)

The Persian poet caught the mood of urgency as old Khayyam shook Sáki's bare shoulder, saying 'Wake up, girl! Wake up!' She turned sleepily, one arm stretched out across the pillow. The morning light – officious hunter of the east– was even now shining through the window. 'Hurry, hurry, we've no time to waste,' he said, and from the tavern opposite they heard the cry:

Awake, my little ones, and fill the cup,
Before Life's liquor in its cup is dry.

Six centuries later, John Donne awoke to the sun's rise and grumbled:

Busy old fool, unruly sun,
Why dost thou thus,
Through windows, and through curtains call on us?

And he told the unwelcome morning light to go away and 'chide late schoolboys and sour prentices', but to leave him alone with his mistress.

'*Surgite! Surgite!*' shouted the duty prefect in Latin, 'Wake up! Wake up!' It was 5am and time for the pupils of Winchester College to start their day. Never did sleepy schoolboy greet dawn with such grudging reluctance as James Woodforde, aged twelve years, in 1759. Struggling to wake from sleep, he joined the others at morning prayers, when it was their custom to sing words written for them by Bishop Ken:

> *Awake, my soul, and with the sun*
> *Thy daily stage of duty run;*
> *Shake off dull sloth, and joyful rise*
> *To pay thy morning sacrifice.*

Whether from the arms of a lover or at the insistent call of an intrusive alarm (busy old fool); whether in answer to habit or duty, or the urgent and untimely demands of guilty pleasure; and whether we wish it or not, our whole world turns inexorably towards the light as we rise once more to face another day.

Each of us devises our strategy by which to navigate the rocks and currents of those early hours. Some make a hearty breakfast, listening to *Today* on Radio 4. Others, pressed for time, grab a cup of coffee, while chivvying the children to get ready for school. Others, in smart hotels, gaze with jaundiced eye upon the Trimalchian feast of cereals, figs, prunes, cold meats, and sizzling mixed grills of bacon, sausage, kidneys and black pudding. Some, driven by who knows what, go on an early run before a shower and the long commute to the office. Others – soldiers, prisoners and children at boarding school – awake to the unceasing clamour of community life. Old people and insomniacs switch on the light and welcome with relief the end of another long and lonely night. Others with nothing left to live for pull up the duvet and wish life would all just go away.

Some of us have found another way of greeting the morning. The Daily Office is a brief spiritual exercise during which texts from the Bible and Christian tradition are recited either privately or corporately: ten minutes of duty (*officium*) first devised by St Benedict fifteen centuries ago. It is a formula that, over the years, has been translated and continually revised to meet the devotional needs of each generation of Christian believers.

As I pray the Office – regularly, though not without lapses, sometimes with feeling, often without fervour, but never without profit – I draw comfort from the knowledge that I am surrounded by that great host of men and women, which no one can number, whose faith is greater than mine and whose quiet persistence in an unbelieving world must surely be a mark of saintliness.

'The night is past and the day lies open before us,' I begin, as our world once more turns towards the light.

ADVENT CALENDAR

Time was when we made our own Advent calendars, cutting them from cardboard and folding those little doors, each opening to reveal a different symbol of Christmas – an angel, a shepherd, a king, a camel and so on – until the final one disclosed the baby Jesus in the manger.

Then, at some point in the last fifty years or so, the iconography changed. Biblical images were replaced by Father Christmas, reindeers, sleighs, robins and snowmen with red noses. Chocolates, too, began to make an appearance behind the doors, bringing the opportunity for parental intervention. 'If you don't behave, you won't open today's door,' or, when things got really bad, 'If you don't stop that silly grizzling, I'll open the door and EAT YOUR CHOCOLATES MYSELF.' Of course, that was before the Elf on the Shelf had made his baleful presence felt.

But those simple days have long gone. Grown-ups have moved in and appropriated the Advent calendar for themselves. Harrods, in 2010, set the bar at its highest by marketing the world's first million-dollar Advent calendar containing, among other goodies, a designer kitchen and an 8.5-metre speedboat. Selfridges, too, has now joined in. For the more modest sum of £500, they are offering this year (2017) their Diptyque calendar, housing twenty-five little surprises for the pampered recipient. These include small bottles of lotion, jars of beauty creams and sundry sweetly scented unguents. Slipping a little lower down the list you will find Liberty's offering: their Beauty Advent Calendar costing a mere £300 (Liberty's, you too? Oh, that it should have come to this!).

But, all the time and still just audible beneath our mad

racket of over-spending, there sounds the solemn warning of Advent, which our Christian forefathers placed with careful deliberation at this time of year. 'Sleepers, wake up!' they cried and repeated the call throughout the four Sundays of Advent, declaring the ancient themes of Christ's Second Coming and the Great Assize.

They heard that sound first on Jordan's bank in John the Baptist's uncompromising call to repent: 'Who warned you to flee from the wrath to come?' We hear it today in the music of our cathedrals and parish churches when the choirs sing the Advent responsory '*Rorate Caeli*': 'Drop down ye heavens from above, and let the skies pour down righteousness'. We hear it in the words of 'Sleepers, Awake', the sixteenth-century German chorale incorporated by J S Bach in his Advent Cantata. And we must be deaf not to hear it in so many Advent hymns, not least in Charles Wesley's 'Lo, He Comes with Clouds Descending', the most explicit statement of the Church's belief in the Second Coming.

Those partygoers heard it too, in carefree, fun-loving Venice. During the eighteenth century, she who once had 'held the gorgeous East in fee', was enjoying a season of parties, not knowing this was to be her last. Suddenly, the revellers felt a chill. They broke off talking and listened to what the hired musician, Baldassaro Galuppi, was playing on the harpsichord, hearing now in his music unwelcome notes of foreboding:

> *What? Those lesser thirds so plaintive, sixths diminished sigh on sigh,*
> *Told them something? Those suspensions, those solutions –*
> *"Must we die?"*
> *Those commiserating sevenths – "Life must last! We can but try!"*

And, try as they might to keep the party going, within two decades Venice had fallen and the fun was over.

As for Venice and its people, merely born to droop and drop,
Here on earth they bore their fruitage, mirth and folly were the crop,
What of soul was left, I wonder, when the kissing had to stop?

"Dust and ashes," so you croak it, and I want the heart to scold,
Dear dead women, with such hair too – what's become of all the gold
Used to hang and brush their bosoms? I feel chilly and grow old.

Robert Browning, *A Toccata of Galuppi's*

O SAPIENTIA

O Wisdom, coming forth from the mouth of the Most High,
filling all creation and reigning to the ends of the earth; come
and teach us the way of truth.

From early times (about the sixth century AD) during the seven days before Christmas the Magnificat at Vespers was introduced and concluded with a special antiphon – a brief passage of scripture indicating the significance of the approaching feast. Each of the seven days had its own antiphon based upon one of the seven titles of Christ: *O Sapientia* (Wisdom); *O Adonai* (Lord of lords); *O Radix Jesse* (Root of Jesse); *O Clavis David* (Key of David); *O Oriens* (Morning Star); *O Rex Gentium* (King of the Nations); and *O Emmanuel* (God with Us). J M Neale's hymn 'O Come, O Come, Emmanuel' recites five of the titles.

Originally, the sequence began on 17th December (O Sapientia) and ended on 23rd (O Emmanuel); the 24th being the Vigil of The Feast of the Nativity and therefore outside Advent.

The English pre-Reformation rite (Sarum Use) had its own variation, according to which the seven Great O's began on the 16th December, bringing the whole sequence forwards by one day. An eighth was then added to the end (23rd December) in honour of Our Lady (*O Virgo Virginum*). Pre-Reformation England was famous for her devotion to Mary and was known as 'Mary's Dowry'. We were also, even then, famous for doing things our way, and therefore falling out of step with the Continent.

At the Reformation, the practice of singing the antiphons

disappeared, but a faint echo remained in the Book of Common Prayer calendar, which retains the words 'O Sapientia' against the 16th December. Cranmer's calendar can still be found in the 1662 Prayer Book.

During the liturgical reforms of 1960–2000, culminating in the Anglican Common Worship, the use of the Advent antiphons was reintroduced as an optional devotion at the Daily Office of Evensong. Our liturgists decided to follow the continental practice and not the English rite, and so O Sapientia now falls on the 17th December – a minor irritation to those Sophies and Sophias born on the 16th whose birthdays and name days no longer coincide.

Holy Wisdom (Hagia Sophia), whom the Church identifies with Christ, tells of her glory in a passage from the pre-Christian text originating in Ptolemaic Egypt and is now included in the Apocrypha under the title 'Ecclesiasticus', or, more correctly, 'The Wisdom of Jesus Ben Sirach':

I came forth from the mouth of the Most High, and covered the earth like a mist. I dwelt in the heavens and my throne was in a pillar of cloud. Alone I compassed the vault of heaven and traversed the depths of the abyss. Over the waves of the sea, over all the earth, and over every people and nation I have held sway.

Ecclesiasticus 24:3–6

WHEN GOD LEAPT DOWN FROM HEAVEN

When peaceful silence lay over all, and night was in the midst
of her swift course: from your royal throne, O God, down
from the heavens, leapt your almighty Word.

Wisdom 18:14,15a

Those words are spoken or sung as an antiphon before and
after the Magnificat at the weekday evening office during
the Christmas season. Our liturgists have rescued them
from the obscurity of medieval Vespers and restored them to
contemporary use; just one of many examples of the riches of
Common Worship.

They come from the Book of Wisdom, which can
be found in the Apocrypha – that strange collection of
scriptures that were not considered sufficiently authoritative
to win their place in the canon of the Old Testament or the
New, but that were thought worthy of retention albeit in a
subordinate rank.

When peaceful silence lay over all, and night was in the midst
of her swift course: from your royal throne, O God, down
from the heavens, leapt your almighty Word.

The unknown author was probably a member of the
Hellenistic Jewish community in Alexandria. Scholars are
uncertain about his dates, and place him somewhere between
late second century BC and early first century AD. Even if
these words were written later than the birth of Christ, it
is thought unlikely that they are a reference to Bethlehem.

They should be understood in the light of contemporary Jewish thought, of which the Alexandrian philosopher Philo was a leading exponent. According to this, there was a close conjunction between the biblical understanding of the divine Word and the Greek idea of the Logos – the rational principle underlying the universe.

> *In the beginning was the Word,* [begins the Christmas Gospel] *and the Word was with God, and the Word was God. He was in the beginning with God. All things came into being through him.*
>
> John 1:1–3

In the beginning came the first Big Bang, when by the Word's utterance the universe came, and still comes, into being. Then came, and still comes, the second Big Bang, when the same almighty Word leapt down from heaven in an explosion of energy that we call the Incarnation (God's great leap).

As in some old vinyl recordings, a strong audio signal creates in advance of itself a faint echo, so the Incarnation set up a pre-echo in the minds of the prophets. When, in the ninth century BC, Isaiah declared, 'Unto us a child is born, unto us a son is given,' he was speaking about the arrival of a national leader who would save Israel from the king of Assyria. But in his words Christ's disciples heard the pre-echo of a greater wonder: the Word made flesh in Palestine.

> *O morning stars, together proclaim the holy birth,*
> *And praises sing to God the King,*
> *and peace to men on Earth.*

IN THE BLEAK MIDWINTER

Christina Rossetti*

(First published in the *Church Times*, 22nd April 2005)

What is the use, Christina, of having a heart like a singing bird and a water shoot and all the rest of it, if you insist on getting yourself up like a pew-opener?

In Max Beerbohm's cartoon an exasperated Dante Gabriel Rossetti rebukes his dowdy sister. And what *was* the use? In the nursery, Christina had been 'a fiery spirit'. In the schoolroom she had played chess to *win*. Why now this self-abasement?

Christina Rossetti grew up, a much-loved daughter and sister in a literary family. Delight in the music of words surrounded her. A month before her fifteenth birthday her health broke. The cause was never stated, though the sickness was mental and physical. The shutters came down. Equipped with a precocious talent, she wrote poems, at first with titles like 'Love and Death', in which doomed lovers elope in a gondola and sink to a watery grave. Later she found her own voice.

In verse of technical inventiveness and luminous diction, she touched upon themes of love and loss. Even her fairy tale *Goblin Market*, with its light 'rippling metre', contained darkly passionate undertones. Here is her description of Lizzie's resistance to the goblins' assault upon her innocence:

White and golden Lizzie stood
Like a lily in a flood...

Like a royal virgin town
Topped with gilded dome and spire
Close beleaguered by a fleet
Mad to tear her standard down.

There was humour too. 'You pulled legs, you tweaked noses', wrote Virginia Woolf. Christina recognised the pew-opener in herself. 'I mean to trim up my old hat in preparation for possible croquet', she wrote, self-mockingly, about a visit to friends in Scotland. In company, she was a pithy conversationalist, with 'a gently caustic tongue'. In solitude, she was haunted by a sense of injury.

There comes a vague alarm,
A shrinking in the memory
From some forgotten harm.

(From The Last Hope)

Religion was her cure, she said. Others thought it was a symptom of her illness. Her brother William compared its effect upon his sisters. Maria became 'serenely happy', but Christina acquired 'an awful sense of unworthiness.' At that time the sisters and their mother regularly attended Christ Church, Albany Street, where the austere Dr Pusey sometimes preached, and a harsh Tractarian discipline was taught.

If others hinted at 'religious mania', she saw it differently: 'I became unbearable to myself... then I found help in confession and absolution and spiritual counsel, and relief inexpressible.'

Marriage eluded her. There was a broken engagement. Later, there was another love. Then she devoted herself to the service of others and to writing. While her father lived, she was his amanuensis. Holman Hunt remembered the old man and his fellow Italian émigrés talking of Garibaldi as the silent daughter stood behind his chair.

When her father died, she applied to join Florence Nightingale at Scutari, but was thought too young. She taught in her mother's school. Later, she worked as a volunteer in a House of Mercy for fallen women. At forty, she succumbed to Graves's disease, a disfiguring affliction. People remembered her youthful beauty, depicted in her brother's painting of the Annunciation, *Ecce ancilla Domini.*

Her brother had asked: What was the use? Christina's passionate nature found, in the bleak midwinter of her life, the fulfilment of a longing that human love had failed to satisfy.

> *My heart is like a singing bird...*
> *Because the birthday of my life*
> *Is come, my love is come to me.*

(From 'A Birthday')

Her love was Jesus Christ.

---

* Christina Rossetti (1830–1899) is the author of the popular Christmas hymn 'In the Bleak Midwinter'.

WHILE SHEPHERDS WATCHED

Nahum Tate (1652–1715)

(Adapted from an article published in the *Church Times*,
20th December 2002)

Nahum Tate, the author of 'While Shepherds Watched Their Flocks by Night', was an unlikely hymn writer. The son of an Irish clergyman called Faithful Teate, he settled in London after the Restoration in 1660, when he changed his name and made a precarious living with his pen. He wrote a number of largely unsuccessful plays, and translated or adapted the works of others.

Apart from his Christmas hymn, his most memorable achievements were to write the libretto for Purcell's *Dido and Aeneas*, and to adapt Shakespeare's *King Lear* by eliminating entirely the role of the fool, and having Edgar marry Cordelia so that they all lived happily ever after. This version was still popular at the beginning of Queen Victoria's reign.

Like many of his trade he led a rackety life. Chronically short of money and harassed by creditors, he produced work far beneath his abilities and took to drink. He did, however, have his successes: King Charles was amused by one of his plays, and his ode 'Panacea – a Poem on Tea' was generally well received.

To the surprise of many, he was appointed Poet Laureate by William III. Southey called him the second worst Laureate ever and Pope made a waspish comment about him in the *Dunciad*. George I declined to re-appoint him, and Tate closed his career by dying suddenly and unexpectedly in the Royal Mint, while seeking refuge from his creditors.

The work by which he is now best known, 'While Shepherds Watched Their Flocks by Night', was probably not one he would have considered highly. It first appeared in 1700 in a supplement to the metrical version of the psalms which he and Nicholas Brady had published in 1696.

Ever since the suppression of carol singing earlier in the 17th century, there had been no authorised Christmas hymn; indeed, there had been no authorised hymns at all, apart from a few exceptions like the Gloria and the Te Deum. Only biblical texts, such as metrical psalms, were thought appropriate for singing in church – or paraphrases of biblical passages such as this one by Tate, which is a metrical version of the Lukan narrative (comparison with Luke 2:8–14 shows how closely he followed the King James Bible).

'While Shepherds Watched…' soon became popular. People now had the chance to sing a carol in church without censure. Its metre matched a large number of popular tunes. One of the first tunes it was sung to was 'St James' ('Thou Art the Way', AMNS 128), but later, during the eighteenth century, it was sung to a number of wonderfully roistering 'Chapel' tunes such as *Northrop* (EH app 8), *Lyngham, Old Foster's* and *Cranbrook*. The last two are still sung as pub carols in Yorkshire, though *Cranbrook* is now better known as the tune for 'On Ilkley Moor Baht 'At'.

It was not until the editors of *Hymns Ancient and Modern* (1861) linked Tate's Christmas hymn to the rather dull little tune known as 'Winchester Old' that the world got used to singing it to its staid 'Church' tune. But what a loss to our carol services has been the ousting of those wild 'Old Methodist' tunes with their repeats and flourishes, and splendid bravura.

Nahum Tate should be remembered for more than just his Christmas hymn. Apart from sparing generations of playgoers the tiresome drolleries of Shakespeare's fool and providing

Purcell with the libretto for *Dido and Aeneas*, he gave us some excellent hymns and fought to liberate Anglican worship from the stale psalmody of its puritan past. He died in obscure poverty: he deserved better.

PROCESSION OF THE MAGI

Evelyn Waugh describes in his novel *Helena* how the Emperor's mother prayed for the great ones; those who, like her son, Constantine, were overloaded with power. She addressed the Magi, not only on behalf of them, but of all late-comers and all who make a laborious journey to the truth, that they might at last find kneeling space in the straw.

We, too, at Epiphany-tide should pray for the captains and the kings of this world, for all who are encumbered with the trappings of rank and all who hold high office in our earthly realms: the potentates and autocrats, the moguls, satraps and the *grands seigneurs*, the honourable and kind as well as the crooks and bullies.

You can see them depicted on the walls of the chapel in the Palazzo Medici in Florence. In Gozzoli's sumptuous murals they appear now more as kings than magi in their gorgeous robes and golden crowns: Melchior, Balthasar and Caspar. The artist brought those legendary figures up to date by depicting them as the three great powers of his time, Sigismund, Emperor of the West; John VIII Palaeologus, Emperor of the East; and Lorenzo the Magnificent, Florentine ruler and patron of the arts. Surrounding and following them is a glorious cavalcade of the great and the good of fifteenth century Florence.

All our solemn processions, choreographed to celebrate the majesty of our secular kingdoms, are now transfigured by those three strange figures, as they come to make their obeisance to a higher king.

The academics are also there. They are the ones who travel cautiously, taking sights and making calculations, moving, despite themselves, towards the simplicity of Bethlehem. They proceed by many detours and reversals, like knights on a chess board, two steps to the side and one step forwards – or sometimes back. How splendid they are in their academic robes: doctors in scarlet and masters in distinct liveries of red, white, purple, blue, green or gold.

Behind them come the shy researchers, overshadowed by their more famous peers, blinking in the bright light of day after too much time spent in the Bodleian or hunting down, like ferrets, their quarry in the back stacks of the London Library. You can be sure that the fruit of their hidden labour will endure, albeit known only to the cognoscenti as footnotes in the published works of lesser scholars. They, too, shall have their place in the sun.

And then there are the delicate ones: exquisite flowers, easily bruised and quick to take offence. Too fastidious for this careless world, they seem to achieve so much less than they once promised, perhaps because they try too hard. They are there, too, though reluctant to be jostled in the crush by so many other unrecognised contenders.

Celebrities of stage and screen are also there, jealous of their fragile reputations. Familiar with exposure in the press, and often not unwilling to be glimpsed leaving a restaurant or attending an awards ceremony. They now follow discreetly, just visible as they pass, seated well back in their limousines, protected by bodyguard and agent (to whom all enquiries must first be made in writing).

The long and splendid procession of the great, the learned, the oblique, the delicate and the famous-for-being-famous passes on its way to Bethlehem.

'Vanity of vanities,' said the preacher, 'all is vanity,' and gave his condescending smile.

But was the preacher right to be so scornful? And did the poet need to remind us of what we already knew:

The glories of our blood and state
Are shadows, not substantial things;
There is no armour against Fate;
Death lays his icy hand on kings:
Sceptre and Crown
Must tumble down,
And in the dust be equal made
With the poor crooked scythe and spade.

James Shirley (1596–1666)

Helena was more gracious than both preacher and poet when she urged the Magi, 'Pray always for all the learned, the oblique, the delicate. Let them not be quite forgotten at the throne of God when the simple come into their kingdom.'

VILLAGE PANTOMIME

The pantomime season is upon us. They have had the auditions for the village production, and rehearsals are well under way. The village show will be a sell-out. It always is.

Village pantomimes are a fairly recent tradition, introduced sometime in the twentieth century, but in London Christmas theatricals have a long pedigree going back to the sixteenth century or earlier. These musical performances were performed as masques before the king and his court at Whitehall, and also before the lawyers and students in their Inns of Court.

Court masques were performed as part of the Twelfth Night celebrations of Christmas, and employed the literary skills of writers such as William Shakespeare and Ben Jonson. Members of the court, including King Charles I and his queen, would join in the performances and dance to the music of court musicians such as William Byrd and Henry Lawes. There was about those occasions an element of topsy-turveydom. It is a noble tradition that still persists: the squire plays the buffoon, the parson forgets his lines and the blacksmith wears drag.

Another feature – the magical effects of scenery changes – derives from the spectacular contribution of Inigo Jones, court architect to the king. His productions were lavish. In 1611, the *Masque of Oberon* cost £2,000, a colossal sum. Ben Jonson, who was paid £40 for the script, complained that the scenery was upstaging the actors. The dramatist and the stage designer had a spat, setting a pattern of theatrical squabbling for future years.

Although court masques were not reintroduced on

the same scale in Whitehall Palace after the Restoration – Oliver Cromwell, unsurprisingly, had banned them – they reappeared in a different guise during the early eighteenth century in Mr Rich's pantomimes at his theatre in Lincoln's Inn Fields. Some of the most familiar elements of this Christmas entertainment – for example, the sudden eruption of the demon king roaring and cackling through a concealed trapdoor – have their origins in the court masque, if not in that earlier manifestation of popular entertainment: the mummers' play.

A basic element of pantomime – the use of the stereotype – derives from the Italian *Commedia dell' Arte* with its recurring characters such as Harlequin, Columbine, Pierrot, Punch and Pantaloon. At the same time as John Rich was producing his pantomime spectaculars in the 1720s, theatre 'in the Italian manner' was enjoying the vogue at Drury Lane. Rich borrowed from this. He also borrowed from the circus.

During the nineteenth century, children's stories and nursery rhymes provided the plots: Dick Whittington, Cinderella and Mother Goose among others, and Harlequin, Columbine, Pierrot and Pantaloon gave way to a new generation of stereotypes, including the young lovers, the dame in drag, the wicked uncle and the fairy godmother.

Meanwhile, in our village celebration, the producer, script-writer, scenery builders, chorus trainer, musical director/choreographer, make-up artists, electrician, sound engineer, wardrobe mistress and performers combine their skills to create for us a spectacle of splendid buffoonery the like of which you would never expect to see again – until next Christmas when the whole gallimaufry is cooked up once more for our delight and reassurance.

CANDLEMAS

(From a sermon preached at the Sung Eucharist at
Withyham parish church at Candlemas, 2009)

Candlemas or, to give it its proper name, the Feast of the Presentation of Christ in the Temple, celebrates the occasion when Mary and Joseph fulfilled the Jewish custom of bringing their firstborn son to the Temple as an act of thanksgiving and dedication.

They were not alone that day. The Temple was a busy place, rather like St Paul's Cathedral on a weekday. There would have been sightseers and Jewish visitors from abroad: members of the diaspora living in the great cities of the empire – Rome, Alexandria and Corinth – many of whom were making their once-in-a-lifetime pilgrimage to Jerusalem. There would have been small groups of people listening to instruction from the rabbis. There would have been individuals trying to find space in their lives for reflection and prayer. And in the distant sanctuary there would have been the chanting and the drift of incense. Outside the doors, in the courtyard, there would have been the noise and chatter of the stall-holders selling pigeons for sacrifice, and the money-changers exchanging the common currency of everyday use (the Roman denarius, ritually unclean, as it bore the image of Caesar) for the Hebrew coinage needed for the Temple fees.

In the midst of all this turbulence entered Joseph and Mary with their child. It was, for them, a very special moment, as it was for every parent on such an occasion. They became aware of an old man approaching them. He seemed to know them. He held out his arms towards the child. Old Simeon was one of those rare people who have the power to see through the surface of events and perceive the underlying truth of what is happening. God bestows on them the gift of prophecy.

'This Child,' said Simeon, 'is the long awaited one – a light to lighten the nations, the glory of God's chosen people, Israel.'

What an extraordinary thing – what a moment in time that was when the old man spoke those words. What a disclosure of grace. And there, in that little group, something was happening of which none of the others in the crowded Temple was at all aware.

Imagine the scene: the thronging tourists and pilgrims, people who had come for so many different reasons – the sick hoping for a cure, the lost looking for a meaning, the weary seeking rest and the bored in search of a wonder. And there, in the middle of them all, unobserved, this private disclosure of truth.

All the stories of Christmas (and this one is part of the Christmas cycle) have this in common. They describe events that happened on the margins of history. The drama unfolds not centre stage but in the wings. The baby is born in the obscurity of a stable, and, except for a few shepherds, no one seemed to know about the birth of God's son. When the Wise Men came looking for the child born to be king, no one in Jerusalem had heard of him.

This reticence, this deliberate concealment by God of his intervention in human history, is characteristic of the Gospel story. At the wedding at Cana, when Jesus turned the water into wine, his action was behind the scenes; only the servants knew. And, when he cured the sick, he would often tell the person whom he had healed not to broadcast what had happened.

The concealment of his true nature seems at first sight rather strange, but it is consistent with the Hebrew tradition that God conveys his truth in parables. When asked why, Jesus quotes the words of Isaiah: that he did not speak in plain statements 'lest in hearing they might not hear, and in seeing they might not understand.' He does not inflict upon our minds the banner headlines of certainty, but rather he whispers in our hearts gentle hints, giving only glimpses of what lies beneath the surface.

He came to his Temple carried in the arms of Mary, but of all the people who saw that little family from Nazareth only one old man and one old woman took notice.

He comes today to this country church in Sussex and quietly discloses himself in the bread and wine. It is a momentous miracle and, like that small group in the Temple, we are few to witness it, while outside this place made holy by his presence our noisy world goes roaring on its way.

THE MEN IN GREY SUITS

(From a sermon preached in St Alban's Church, Wood Street,
on Easter Day, 2004)

On Friday, we remembered the death of Jesus on a cross. Today, we celebrate his resurrection – his rising from the tomb. Between the two events something very important happened. Something precious and honourable was done to prepare his body for burial, and it was done by two men who played an almost hidden role in the Gospel story.

These two men were secret admirers of our Lord. They were undeclared disciples: undecided, covert. They were members of the ruling council (the Sanhedrin), which had decided to arrest Jesus and bring about his death. Joseph of Arimathaea had not voted with the others. We are not told whether Nicodemus did or not. What we do know is this: Jesus's death converted both of them from secret admirers into open disciples.

As soon as he could, Joseph hurried round to Pilate's headquarters and asked the governor for permission to take the body down from the cross for burial. Just think for a moment what that meant. Here was a well-to-do member of the council making a public gesture of support and respect for a disgraced and executed criminal. We can imagine the circumstances. Nothing could have been more dangerous than publicly removing the body from the place of execution and burying it in a tomb that had been prepared for himself.

And then there was Nicodemus. He was the one who had come to Jesus under cover of darkness two or three years earlier. He had been drawn to the Galilean, but was uncertain and, understandably, afraid. But now he came to help, bringing with him the linen and spices necessary for burying Jesus's body. According to St John's account, Nicodemus brought a mixture of aloes and myrrh; a large amount weighing about a hundred pounds (45 kilograms) fit for the burial of a king.

Consider what these two men risked by making this reckless gesture. They faced possible arrest and disgrace. It is tantalising that the Bible tells us so little about them. They hover on the margins. They were clearly well respected by the early Church. The way they are referred to in the story suggests that they were sufficiently well known to be recognised by the first listeners to the Gospel texts.

What was it that made them declare themselves so publicly as followers of the crucified Jesus? And why so soon? Remember this: they did not know then that Jesus would rise again. All they knew was that he had died. It was his death, not his resurrection, that converted them. These two men in grey suits, cautious and circumspect, had become the first converts to the crucified Christ.

Well, not quite the first. There was another: the Roman centurion who had commanded the execution squad. He was a man who doubtless had seen many such executions in his time, but this one was different. According to the Gospel narrative, he was the first person to be drawn by Jesus's death. We are told that, when he saw how Jesus died, he exclaimed, 'Truly, this man was the Son of God.' Tradition gave him a name, Longinus, and ascribed to him a martyr's crown. How much of Longinus's later story was legend we do not know, but that need not obscure the important role he played in the Gospel story.

These three men – Joseph of Arimathaea, Nicodemus and Longinus – were the first to fulfil Jesus's own words when he said, 'I, when I am lifted up from the earth, will draw all people unto me.'

HALLELUIAH CHORUS

Handel confessed that when he composed his 'Halleluiah Chorus' he did so under the influence of overwhelming emotion. 'I did think I did see all heaven before me, and the great God himself.'

That intense feeling can be heard in the music, so that generations of listeners and performers have been able to catch a glimpse of Handel's vision of heaven open before them, revealing the great God himself.

There is a mystery in musical composition that is not shared by the visual arts. When painters or sculptors create their work, they transmit by their own hand their vision on to paper, canvas, wood or stone. They are in control of each stage in the process of creation, and so what you see or touch is their creation and theirs alone.

But musical composition is different. The composer creates the beginning of a process, but has no control over its completion. Handel transmitted his vision of heaven on to pieces of paper, which he covered with the dots and squiggles of a musical score. For the performance of that music, he depended on a collection of instrumentalists and singers to do their best to make the music happen. And sometimes their best was not very good.

The very first time anyone heard Handel's *Messiah* – and this was before its first performance, which was in Dublin – it was sung by the Chester Cathedral Choir. Handel complained about their shortcomings. And the very last time he heard his masterpiece sung was by the Tunbridge Wells Ladies' Music Circle. It was not good. When he died a week later, he was still complaining.

There is a notion that, somewhere in an ideal world, there exists the perfect performance of the 'Halleluiah Chorus'. In an *ideal* world, perhaps. What we do know is that there never has been and never will be in this real-but-imperfect world the golden and definitive performance. That being the case, you might think that the truly definitive performance can be found nowhere except in the mind of the composer.

But there is a flaw in this argument. The composer's mind cannot contain the finished performance. He needs the co-operation of others: trumpets and tenors, oboes, altos, strings, bassoons, and all that great conjunction of wind, percussion, brass, wood, valves, stops, bows, sticks, lungs, breath, diction, lips and teeth. Even the most sublime music must have its physical and mechanical incarnation.

In Christ we have been given the one true performance of the Creator's vision of humanity. For this one and only time, the performance of the artist's intention is both ideal and real, and happens in an imperfect world.

And in Easter we are given a glimpse of humanity's resurrection. When Jesus was raised by God on the third day, he left behind an empty tomb. Not only his spirit but also the physical and mechanical structure of an entire human life has been transformed and raised to glory.

Our Easter faith is this: that what God has done for Jesus, he will do for all our human race – and that includes you, me, the Chester Cathedral Choir, and all members past and present of the Tunbridge Wells Ladies' Music Circle.

Halleluiah! Halleluiah!

TRINITY SUNDAY

(A sermon preached in Guildford Cathedral
on Trinity Sunday, 1987)

A child inhabits an enclosed world. It is a world that, to his way of thinking, relates only to himself. It has no existence independent of himself. Other people are there only insofar as they impinge upon him. Mother, father, brother and sister fit into the scheme of things precisely and exclusively as *his* mother, *his* father, *his* brother or *his* sister. They have no other roles to play except to comfort and to protect, or to threaten and dismay the little person at the centre of the universe, from whom all existence derives its purpose.

But the child in the nursery grows up. One summer evening, after he has been tucked up in bed and kissed goodnight, after the shades have been drawn down upon his busy world, he hears laughter and voices in the garden beneath his window. Going to the window, he watches unobserved, as his beloved parents stroll up and down the lawn, arm in arm, talking and laughing, and now and then stopping to pull up a weed from the border or breathe in the scent of the honeysuckle on the trellis.

To the silent observer, a door is opened in his mind. For the first time, he sees his parents enjoying a life independent of him. He is not the centre of their lives. Moving through the door, he knows that something deep within him has changed for ever.

Trinity Sunday opens a door to us and we glimpse God in his splendour, as he is, independent of us his children. We catch sight of a dimension of being independent of the contingencies of this little world and all its attention-seeking ways. Of all the major festivals of the Church's calendar, there is only one that is not in one way or another a reflection of human need. The great festivals of Christmas, Epiphany, Easter and Whitsun all celebrate God's actions towards the human race. They inevitably picture the Almighty in terms of what he has done for us, his children. The Feast of the Blessed and Undivided Trinity, however, opens for us a door in heaven, and discloses a vision of unimaginable beauty and endless joy: the vision of God as he is in his infinite being, transcending the narrow limits of our nursery world with all its self-centred anxieties and needs.

You and I need to dwell upon this vision. We need to attune our ears to the sound of that great angelic chorus of praise, lest we allow the discordant clamour of this world's problems to deafen us to that ultimate harmony wherein alone they find their resolution.

Of course, we must care about this world. Of course, we must introduce this care into our worship by interceding for its needs. But intercession must be subordinate to praise, otherwise our liturgy degenerates into a sort of fussy humanitarianism. Our inclination to pack our prayers with detailed lists of all that is wrong with society, at home and abroad and to fill our calendars with days of prayer for this, weeks of prayer for that and vigils of prayer for the other – all of which suggests that poor old God is hard of hearing – is symptomatic of our loss of faith in God and his divine providence. We are in danger of reverting to the nursery, of becoming not the Church Militant, but the Church Petulant.

The Feast of the Holy Trinity, then, corrects this tendency by opening a door in heaven to us, through which we can catch a glimpse of God's glory and hear the sound of angels. It reminds us that our best way of approaching the divine mystery of God's being is through worship. The eternal community of love that is the Holy Trinity is not to be apprehended by logical explanation. It is not a problem that has to be solved. As long as we think of the Holy Trinity as a mathematical problem that must be elucidated by experts, we will continue to miss the point. Anyway, it is not very polite. Your best friend would not like to think that you regarded him or her as a problem needing to be explained.

The Holy Trinity of God is experienced in worship, not apprehended by reason. We are prompted by the Holy Spirit at work in our hearts to reach up to the glory of the Father as revealed to us in the life, death and resurrection of the Son, Jesus Christ our Lord. Each prayer, whether it be expressed in the formal structure of a collect, or whether it is the spontaneous and non-verbal yearning of the soul for her creator, is caught up into the dynamic that is the inner life of God. We pray to the Father, through the Son and in the power of the Holy Spirit. We go through the door that is opened for us and pass into heaven, into the very life of the triune God to whom is ascribed, as is most justly due, all might, dominion, majesty and power, henceforth and for ever.

ONWARD CHRISTIAN SOLDIERS

Sabine Baring-Gould

(First published in the *Church Times,* 27th December 2013)

Sabine Baring-Gould was born in 1834 into a West Country family, who had held the manor and patronage of Lew Trenchard in Devon for many generations. Known now chiefly as the author of the hymn *Onward Christian Soldiers,* he was, in his time, a widely read author on Church history, theology, folklore, archaeology and hymns. His *Lives of the Saints* ran to fifteen volumes. He wrote forty novels. However, he regarded his principal role as that of priest and pastor, culminating in forty-three years of service as Rector of Lew Trenchard. He died on 2nd January 1924.

He carried his great height with a patrician's bearing. Some people found him aloof. He avoided society. He disliked clergy gatherings and had a low opinion of bishops. Of the troublesome Archbishop of York, William Thomson, he wrote that 'He possessed an autocratic temper, such as was naturally bred in a man rapidly advanced from a breeches-maker's shop in a small provincial town.' Confident of his heritage and vocation, Baring-Gould needed to look for no advancement beyond his rectory.

Serving as curate in Horbury in Yorkshire, he was asked to establish a mission in 'the Brig', the roughest part of the parish. He found a cottage to rent, turning the ground floor into a weekday-night school for adults and the upstairs into a chapel. On Sunday afternoons, there was catechism for the children and choir practice. On Sunday evenings, there was Evensong led by Baring-Gould, immensely tall in his black cassock, and standing on the fender in the upper room; the mantlepiece behind him carrying cross and candles. It was for the children of this congregation that he wrote *Onward Christian Soldiers*, to be sung at the Whit procession.

'You must tell us a story afore you go!' the children would plead, holding him back after the service. He had a great gift for storytelling. Before ordination, he had spent some years on the staff of Hurstpierpoint College in Sussex. Former pupils recalled his pony 'Bottlethrush', which he had brought back from Iceland, and the tame bat that lodged in his room. But, above all, they recollected 'those yarns he used to spin'.

His parishioners in Horbury Brig were colliers, bargemen, miners and mill-hands. He had them in mind when he wrote in his autobiographical novel *Through Flood and Flame*, 'You have not far to look before you find souls so lovely... that you will be convinced it is not in the conservatories of the rich alone that God delights to grow his lilies.'

He fell in love with a sixteen-year-old mill-worker, Grace Taylor, whom, against the wishes of both families, he married two years later. 'A woman's love burns slowly, with great warmth and light, but steadily', he wrote in *Through Flood and Flame*. 'A man's love rages hot and furious, and consumes fuel and furnace.' When Grace died fifty years later, he had engraved on her tomb '*Dimidium animae meae*' ('Half my soul').

She bore him fifteen children. Baring-Gould sometimes lost count. 'And whose little girl are you, my dear?' he asked during a party when the rectory was full of other people's children. 'I'm yours, Daddy.'

In Lew Trenchard, early in the morning, his coachman would bring round the trap and the rector would set off on his rounds, visiting the cottages and, in winter, taking bowls of hyacinth bulbs with the promise to return when they were in bloom. He fixed bells to the pony's harness when driving round his estate to give his men warning, as he did not wish to find them idling. 'He thought it was best so,' said his churchwarden, Charlie Davy, and added, 'Everybody loved him.'

A visiting bishop made a fuss about carrying the cross in procession – a Romish practice in the bishop's opinion. 'Leave it behind the door,' he ordered. Baring-Gould complied, but not before he had instructed the choir to sing an amended version of the processional hymn 'Onward Christian Soldiers'. Instead of the words 'With the Cross of Jesus going on before,' they sang, 'With the Cross of Jesus left behind the door'. Baring-Gould later denied this story, but it stuck.

In a letter to Charlie Davy Baring-Gould, aged eighty-six years, he wrote:

When I came here as rector forty years ago, I had two objects in view, to teach the people of Lew to love God, and to be true to His Catholic Church. I feel deeply how little I have effected through my own shortcomings. But I trust that at the Last Day... you and some others here will be able to speak a word for me. So, dear Charlie, you see I lean on you as my advocate at the last.

Few of his parishioners would have agreed with such a low self-assessment.

CATHEDRAL EVENSONG

One winter afternoon in the 1770s, the Reverend William Richardson wandered into York Minster during weekday Evensong and had a vision. He wrote the following:

> *The gloom of the evening, the rows of candles fixed upon the pillars in the nave, the lighting of the chancel, the two distant candles glimmering like stars on the altar, the sound of the organ, the voices of the choir... had an amazing effect upon my spirits as I walked to and fro in the nave. The varied tones, sometimes low, sometimes swelling into a great harmonious sound, seemed to anticipate the songs of the blessed and the chorus of praise around the throne of God and the Lamb.*

This unexpected experience persuaded Richardson to take a long look at his ministry, which till then had been that of a conventional eighteenth-century parson. In due course he became one of the most effective preachers York had known since the Reformation.

What was it that so moved him that winter afternoon? It could not have been the warmth of the welcome he received from the cathedral clergy, the accessibility of the worship, the topical relevance of the prayers, a sense of participation in the proceedings or, indeed, anything now normally regarded as essential to effective liturgy. All these things were noticeably absent.

Richardson, the casual observer, was left alone. He was allowed to keep his distance. The music, the words of the psalms, the procession of the choir and the building itself were sufficient channels of God's grace.

We should not be surprised. After all, it was in the ancient equivalent of St Paul's Cathedral that Isaiah had his vision, when he saw the Lord sitting upon a throne, high and lifted up, and the train of his robe filling the temple. The distant choir, the slow ritual and the ornaments of the sanctuary furnished the vision that inaugurated his ministry. And, centuries later, old Zachary's encounter with the Archangel Gabriel on the right side of the altar of incense seems to have happened in circumstances not unlike those of a weekday cathedral Evensong on an afternoon in late September. Both these men experienced, in a very public place, an intensely private vision of the awesome and the transcendent.

Churches are sacred places where visions sometimes happen, and so it is a shame if we allow the bustle and intrusive jollity of contemporary worship to crowd out opportunities for detachment and reflection. Many casual visitors are alienated by what they find in church on Sunday. They are the uncommitted and the tentative. Their desire for God, if they admit to such a conscious desire at all, is no more than a very tender seedling, which cannot withstand the friendly attention of well-meaning clergy or the demands of corporate worship. Their diffident faith soon withers in the bright-and-breezy climate of the Parish Communion.

On 3rd March 1775, about the same time as William Richardson had his vision in the Minster, one of the cathedral clergy, the precentor, William Mason, was writing to his friend Horace Walpole. He lamented the tedium of his intermittent duty at the Minster – three months' 'residence' in every twelve – when he was obliged to attend daily worship where 'the ancient maiden gentlewomen and decayed tradesmen of this famous city of York mumble their matins and their vespers'.

How surprised the precentor would have been had he known that standing in the shadows of the great nave not far from where he sat in his cushioned stall was someone who was transported by what he saw there and heard: 'The songs of the blessed and the chorus of praise around the throne of God and the Lamb.'

MELCHIZEDEK AND THE WIDER PICTURE

Whenever we Christians get uppity about the status of our religion *vis-à-vis* other faiths, we should remember Melchizedek.

Melchizedek is a mysterious figure who appears briefly in the Bible, hovering on the margin between fable and history (Genesis 14:18–20). He was the Canaanite king and high priest of Salem who had an encounter with the patriarch Abraham. We are told that he greeted the patriarch with bread and wine, and blessed him. Abraham responded by offering Melchizedek a tithe of his possessions.

At first sight, that might not seem at all unusual. It was the sort of *quid pro quo* you would expect between a landowner and a priest. Just think of all the great captains and kings of Israel – among them Saul, David and Solomon – did they not all receive a blessing from their priest, who in turn conferred a sacred validation of their authority?

But there was something different about Melchizedek. He did not belong; certainly not to Abraham's clan. He was a foreigner. An outsider. A later generation would have called him a gentile. It is not even clear that he worshipped the same God: in his blessing Melchizedek uses the name 'God Most High', but the term usually used by Abraham was 'The Lord God', which is a translation of 'Yahweh' or 'He Who Is'. Melchizedek stood outside the sacred covenant between Yahweh and Abraham. He was not party to the basic institution of Judaism. And yet, here he was, consecrating the patriarch of God's chosen people even before the first of the covenants had been established.

Many centuries later, when the Davidic Kingdom had

been established at Jerusalem (the new name for Salem), one of the coronation hymns (Psalm 110) declares that the newly anointed king was a 'Priest for ever after the order of Melchizedek' – he was being invested with the priestly status of a kingship, which anteceded the patriarchal covenants.

Melchizedek appears for a third and last time in the Epistle to the Hebrews. It is much more than a passing reference. The writer devotes the whole of the seventh chapter to the importance of Melchizedek. He describes the role of Jesus Christ by quoting the ancient coronation hymn: Christ is 'a priest for ever after the order of Melchizedek'. His priesthood does not derive from the Aaronic priesthood, nor is it validated by his Jewish descent. Ultimately, so the writer claims, God's saving grace, as found in Christ, works in a wider sphere than the closed system of the Abrahamic and Mosaic Covenants, or, we might add, the closed system of the Christian Church.

'God moves in a mysterious way his wonders to perform'. Not least of his wonders is the Church – a fractured and blemished institution that, despite all appearances to the contrary, we dare to call the Body of Christ, and through which we have access to our heavenly Father. But, being the beneficiaries of his generosity, it behoves us to remember that he has other wonders to perform beyond the boundaries of our faith. As he said, he has other sheep to care for. He is the Lord of all and has channels of grace other than those given to us by our religion.

After all, Christ is not owned by his Church. He represents a greater constituency, for he is a priest for ever after the order of Melchizedek.

IN PRAISE OF POETS

(From a sermon preached in Holy Trinity Church, Guildford on 16th
September 2005, during the Guildford Book Festival)

I was looking for a copy of Ian Bradley's *Penguin Book of
Christmas Carols* in the Piccadilly branch of Waterstone's.
Approaching the woman at the information desk, I asked,
'Where will I find Christmas carols?' 'Fiction,' she said, and in
one word consigned two thousand years of Christianity to the
realm of make-believe.

But you can see her point, can't you? After all, you could
hardly call *I Saw Three Ships Come Sailing In* factual. But, on
the other hand, you cannot call it fiction. It is neither. It is
metaphor. Metaphor is the stuff of poetry, as it is the stuff of
religion. But our culture gobbles up facts with a greed that is
impatient of metaphor. It wants the facts – just the facts.

Society has a disposition to discount metaphor. In our
utilitarian culture the poet, like the priest, is thought to be one
of life's ornaments. Pretty, but useless. Some would say 'pretty
useless'.

As children, you and I crossed and recrossed with ease
the boundary between fact and fiction, between truth and
fantasy. It was an easy journey to make because the boundary
was soft, and we could bend it to our will. We had not yet
learnt to make a hard distinction between fact and fiction
(or, rather, between fact and metaphor). In our innocence,
facts did not intimidate. Facts were pliable. They had the
power to delight. They had not lost their glory. Bliss it was
that dawn to know that the Bactrian camel had two humps
and the Arabian but one. There was magic in a world that

43

could contain such diversity of ungulates – and there was magic, too, in a language that could contain such a word as 'ungulate'.

But, then, we grew up. And part of growing up, we were told, was to acquire the habit of distinguishing fact from fantasy, rhyme from reason. I believe it is the poet's and the priest's task to reconnect what our wounded world has put asunder. And metaphor is the healing agent. The poet creates new metaphors so that we can enter fully into the reality of daily life. The poem is not an invitation to escape, but an introduction to enter a more vivid truth.

Redemption

Having been tenant long to a rich Lord,
Not thriving, I resolved to be bold,
And make a suit unto him, to afford
A new small-rented lease, and cancel th' old.

In heaven at his manor I him sought:
They told me there that he was lately gone
About some land, which he had dearly bought
Long since on earth, to take possession.

I straight returned, and knowing his great birth,
Sought him accordingly in great resorts:
In cities, theatres, gardens, parks and courts.
At length I heard a ragged noise and mirth
Of thieves and murderers: there I him espied,
Who straight, Your suit is granted, said and died.

In this poem, written four hundred years ago, George Herbert places Christ in the streets of London. Readers would have known well the city's theatres, gardens, parks and courts.

This was Jacobean London in all its turbulence. Webster's *Duchess of Malfi* was playing at the Globe; King James kept court at Whitehall Palace; the archbishop, George Abbot, was at Lambeth; and, further down the Thames, Ben Jonson was drinking with his friends at the Mermaid Tavern. Only a stone's throw away they could hear, from the crowded alleys and stews of Southwark, 'the ragged noise and mirth of thieves and murderers.'

Locating Christ in our own town, the poet creates in our minds a double shock. He compels us to see afresh the meaning of Christ's redeeming death and then, by superimposing the Cross upon the streets we know so well, he makes us see afresh the world for which he died.

During this book festival, it is right that we should honour our writers. I was asked, for the purposes of this sermon, to single out our poets, though what I have said is also true of novelists and biographers. For it is they who reconnect us with our imagination. It is they who shock and startle and delight. And, in doing so, they create tremors in the mind that enable us to enter more fully into life. Without them, we would all be immeasurably the poorer.

For books and their writers, for poetry and its creators, thanks be to God.

LIFE IN A GEORGIAN RECTORY

(First published in *Save Our Parsonages Newsletter*, June 2013)

Of course, not everyone wants to live in a nine-bedroom Georgian rectory. We did, and we loved it. Seven years ago, we moved into Withyham Rectory (East Sussex), and we thoroughly enjoyed our time there until my retirement in April 2013.

Strictly speaking, it was not a Georgian rectory. It had been built in the late seventeenth century on what is believed to have been the same site as its medieval predecessor. Sometime in the eighteenth century the handsome, but unpretentious, house was aggrandised with a classical facade clamped on to its front elevation of nine bays, and its plain front door embellished with a grandiose canopied porch.

Nor did we have nine bedrooms. Thirty years ago, the south wing was sealed off and leased as a separate dwelling. Still, we rubbed along happily enough in these reduced circumstances, making do with five bedrooms, one bathroom, two reception rooms, kitchen, study and a Georgian plunge bath (more of that later).

We treasured the rectory! And so did, and do, the parishioners, who are proud to call it theirs, and no amount of talk about its being benefice property can persuade them otherwise. The great hall, which occupies the ground floor of the central three bays of the house, was a useful venue for parochial church council (PCC) meetings, Bible study, children's choir practice, church social events and an annual deanery chapter dinner. It was also our family dining hall on high days and holidays, such as Christmas, Easter and birthdays. At family celebrations, the grandchildren had space to romp as the adults in mellow and indulgent mood enjoyed their port and cheese. Every Thursday evening in term-time the stately hall would echo with the voices of the children's choir practising choruses for the family service and belting out action songs such as *Oranges and Lemons, The Farmer's in His Den* or even *A Hunting We Will Go.*

Originally the hall had been very much a working space with its great beams exposed to view, roughly plastered walls, stone floor and an open fireplace, which was wide enough to take great branches of timber five-feet long. It was here that local farmers came in muddy boots to pay their tithes, and it was here the rector conducted business with his glebe manager and outdoor staff. Later, in the eighteenth century, the rough walls were panelled and a false ceiling was suspended to hide the beams, bringing the great hall into the home life of the rectory. This process of domestication was carried on into the twentieth century, when the stone flags were replaced with parquet flooring and central heating radiators were installed; both alterations highly regrettable, but judged to be necessary concessions to modern standards of comfort.

The living quarters occupied the north wing, with the panelled (seventeenth-century linen-fold) drawing room at the front and double doors communicating with what used to be the dining room at the back. The doors could be folded back to make the two rooms into one. Above them, on the first floor, there used to be a similar arrangement, creating a large, double reception room, or library and upstairs drawing room. The layout was changed, probably in the early twentieth century.

The kitchen quarters – with servants' hall, kitchen, pantry, scullery and well – occupied the ground floor of the south wing. Sleeping quarters for the rector and his family were on the first floor of the south wing and above the great hall. The servants slept in rooms in the spacious attic or in a small sixteenth-century building next door.

This original disposition of rooms was altered completely when the south wing was closed off and leased in the twentieth century. The north wing now had to accommodate a new kitchen in what had been the dining room, and a bathroom and lavatory upstairs in what had been bedrooms. Until modern times, there had been, of course, no indoor plumbing upstairs. We never discovered where the indoor privy had been before the nineteenth century, if, indeed, there had been one at all. A consequence of this rearrangement was the loss, to the rector and his wife, of all those small 'utility' rooms and cupboards, now out of reach in the south wing. Despite living in such a spacious home, we had nowhere to put the vacuum cleaner, the broom, the brush and pan, and the ironing board. Still, that was a small price to pay.

So far, I have not mentioned the study – and what a study! During my time in sundry parsonages and cathedral houses, I have been lucky in having been provided with excellent studies, all with enough fitted shelves to accommodate an adequate working library. The one in Withyham Rectory, however, exceeded all. With its built-in wall cupboards, deep enough to conceal an overhead projector, screen, guillotine, archived documents and shoe boxes full of old sermons, and its floor-to-ceiling shelving on three walls it was – and is – a study to die for. An additional and charming feature was the fireplace with its Minton-tiled surround.

Finally, the most unusual feature of the rectory was the Georgian plunge bath, installed by a predecessor in the eighteenth century. This was a small, subterranean, stone-lined chamber, four-feet square, the access to which was by a short flight of steps descending beneath the main staircase. Still in place, but no longer in use, were two massive taps, one for cold water and the other for hot. These would have been fed by pipes running beneath the ground to the water supply and the boiler in the south wing. The chamber would have been filled to a depth of four feet, enabling the rector to submerge himself during his daily ablutions. We never discovered which of the past rectors, or his wife, was the last to enjoy this luxury.

A GREEK HAT

There are times when a hat can give the wrong signal. In 175 BC Jason, the renegade High Priest in Jerusalem, collaborated with the Hellenist King Antiochus Epiphanes by causing his young men 'to wear the Greek hat'. This was in clear defiance of Jewish custom. What made matters worse, Jason 'took delight in establishing a gymnasium right under the citadel' in Jerusalem★, and encouraged his clergy to engage in wrestling and other forms of athletics. As it was customary in the ancient games for athletes to compete in the nude, it was not surprising that this behaviour offended Jewish tradition.

Scholars are not sure about the design of the offending hat, whether it was the Phrygian cap or the wide-brimmed *petasos,* but what is certain is that it was identified so closely with the Hellenist oppressors of Judaism that to wear it was a mark of apostasy.

Trousers were another problem. When Shadrach, Meshach and Abednego were thrown into the fiery furnace at the command of Nebuchadnezzar, they were wearing coats, hosen (trousers) and hats. Now that is not how you would expect a Hebrew to be dressed. Trousers were never part of his wardrobe. Can you imagine Moses wearing trousers? Or Elijah? Of course not. The very idea is absurd. Jews in those days wore robes. Trousers were for Babylonians.

What we have in the story of Nebuchadnezzar's fiery furnace is evidence of collaboration, of adopting the local dress code in defiance of Hebrew custom. Their collaboration went further than trousers. The three heroes of the fiery furnace had changed their names too. On receiving senior appointments in the Babylonian civil service – they were well in with the authorities, as was their friend Daniel – they adopted the foreign names of Shadrach, Meshach and Abednego to replace their Hebrew names: Hananiah, Azariah and Mishael. Daniel, too, was given a Babylonian name, but 'Belteshazzar' never seemed to catch on.

Such signs of collaboration, you might agree, are a comfort to us today. We live in a world that requires us to make daily concessions to public opinion – a public opinion that is, at best, indifferent to our faith and, at worst, derisively hostile. We are reassured to know that even Daniel and the heroic three trimmed their sails to the wind. They adjudged their situation carefully. They, loyal Jews in a gentile society, had to decide when it was right to give way and when to stand firm. As we know, when they were asked to bend too far, they declared, 'Thus far, and no further,' and faced the fiery furnace and the lions' den.

The casual expletive 'Christ' or 'Jesus' often heard in conversation still makes me wince, however commonplace it has become. Even so, I doubt that offensive language figures prominently, if at all, in the recording angel's ledger of sins. We used to be more punctilious. In a former generation, penitents were supplied with lists of offences by which to measure their spiritual health. It was after examining one of those fearsome catalogues, which included sins one would never even have known about, that an over-scrupulous nun felt obliged to confess to her priest that she had been troubled by a passing inclination to cut Nones. 'How many times?' he asked. 'Twice since my last confession,' she replied.

Although we are now less scrupulous in these matters, there still remains some uneasiness. I was never sure about my own reaction to the Monty Python film *The Life of Brian*. How far should I have enjoyed such a display of blasphemy? When we excused ourselves, as we usually did, by claiming that what we were laughing at was not the Gospel itself, but a parody of the Gospel, were we not being disingenuous? After all, the whole point of the film, and the reason we thought it was so screamingly funny, was precisely because it *was* a blatant blasphemy, a bit of daring naughtiness, normally off-limits, and something we could giggle at when the grown-ups were out of the room. Not that I agreed with those who tried to get the film banned, but I now think that I should have been more honest at the time. When I saw it again recently, it struck me as not really all that funny, and the reason for that is that forty years later blasphemy of that fairly innocent sort has now become so commonplace it has lost its power to shock or even to amuse. It no longer carries the same frisson of naughtiness. I doubt that anyone now would think of making such a film.

At what point does our collaboration with the customs and attitudes of society become a betrayal of the Gospel? When should we abjure the Greek hat?

*See in the Apocrypha, 2 Maccabees 4:1–16.

ST GILBERT OF SEMPRINGHAM 1083–1189

(First published in the *Church Times*, February 2011)

When they told the failing but once-great king Henry II, beleaguered now by his rebellious sons, that Gilbert of Sempringham had died, he cried out, 'Truly I now know that he has left this life, for these troubles have come upon me because he no longer lives.' It says much about the character of both men that the 'holy man of Sempringham' had not feared to take Becket's side against the king, helping him on one occasion to escape to France, and that the king had pardoned him and become his patron.

Piety, and the confidence that comes with a strong faith, marked his character. Gilbert once bought from a child some spinning tops to distract and calm his companions, when they trembled at the threat of Angevin reprisal. He could be affable, but he had always been a hard and austere master. When, in his earlier years, he ran a parish school, he forbade the boys from 'jesting and wandering about at will'. They did not disobey. On one occasion he struck a recalcitrant canon. But, at his death, he was mourned as 'a father and pastor, a brother and friend' (*Vita* [Life] c1202).

Although he was alive to the distractions of sex – as a young clergyman, he had been troubled by dreams about his landlord's daughter and had felt compelled to change his lodgings – he established joint communities of men and women. Despite one notorious scandal, this experiment was successful during his lifetime, and by his death there were nine double communities. However, by 1300, the 'Gilbertine experiment was largely dead… the canons were everywhere dominant, and the nuns were sidelined' (Brian Golding, *Gilbert of Sempringham,* 1995).

Gilbert's more lasting legacy is in his contribution to that pastoral and domestic spirituality that has been one of the enduring features of the English Church. His first community of women was rooted in the village of Sempringham and in the life of the parish church. The rule he later adapted, based on that of the Augustinian canons, encouraged its members to engage in pastoral work. The Gilbertine houses were subject to episcopal authority (his request to bring them into the Cistercian fold had been rejected), thus ensuring that they remained anchored within the secular church.

Gilbert and the Gilbertine Order have their place in the unobtrusive stream of English spirituality, which runs from Anselm in the eleventh century, through Richard Rolle, Walter Hilton, Julian of Norwich and Margery Kempe, and, later, after the Reformation, resurfaces at Nicholas Ferrars's Little Gidding and George Herbert's Bemerton, then in the nineteenth century at Keble's vicarage and parish church at Hursley, and in the twentieth century in the pastoral ministry and writings of Bill Vanstone.

It was said that, in a dream, a member of Thomas Becket's household had addressed the archbishop with the words, 'There was never anyone in our land, and never will be, to give such rejoicing as you'; flattery, which Becket gruffly contradicted with one word, 'Gilbert.'

THE GLORY OF THE GARDEN

'If I could see the furniture of your heart', wrote William Gilpin to William Mason, 'I should see lawns and flowering shrubs, winding paths and temples, hanging up in golden frames.'

These two eighteenth-century gentlemen, both in holy orders, were discussing garden design. Gilpin did not approve of Mason's mannered designs. The landscape, he said, should be full of blasted oaks and gnarled elms, craggy rocks, grottoes, and leaping cataracts. To which Mason replied that man was not intended to live among lakes and rocky mountains. He held it not amiss, he said, that in his heart there should be seen not the wild scenery of untamed nature, but the domestic landscape of an English garden.

These two men represented contrasting fashions. William Gilpin, as early as 1748, pioneered the theory of the picturesque. By adding to the scenery such accessories as 'gothick' ruins, man-made waterfalls and grottoes, it was intended to heighten the raw effects of Nature.

William Mason, however, approved of Nature only in so far as she had been chastened by Art. In the words of another friend, Horace Walpole, 'The open country was but a canvas upon which a landscape might be designed.' The sight of crude Nature, unfinished by Art, would make one shudder, as it did the eighteenth-century aesthete who, when travelling through the Lake District, averted his eyes from the rugged scene and drew down the carriage blinds.

Ours is a world that no longer permits us to draw down the blinds. Nor, when you come to think of it, was the attempt to do so ever more than affectation. Adam was a gardener and we are all Adam. He prefigures and embodies the human race. As St Paul put it, 'We are of the earth, earthy.' We are gardeners, not observers, and are placed here, as Adam was in Eden, to care for, to weed and prune, to create and preserve the glory of the garden.

As Rudyard Kipling wrote:

Our England is a garden, and such gardens are not made
By singing 'Oh, how beautiful!' and sitting in the shade...
Then seek your job with thankfulness and work till further
orders,
If it's only netting strawberries or killing slugs on borders;
And when your back stops aching and your hands begin to
harden,
You will find yourself a partner in the Glory of the Garden.
Oh, Adam was a gardener, and God who made him sees
That half a proper gardener's work is done upon his knees,
So when your work is finished, you can wash your hands
and pray
For the Glory of the Garden, that it may not pass away.
And the Glory of the Garden it shall never pass away!

COMPLACENCIES OF THE PEIGNOIR

Complacencies of the peignoir, and late
Coffee and oranges in a sunny chair,
And the green freedom of a cockatoo
Upon a rug mingle to dissipate
The holy hush of ancient sacrifice.
She dreams a little, and she feels the dark
Encroachment of that old catastrophe,
As a calm darkness among water-lights.
The pungent oranges and bright, green wings
Seem things in some procession of the dead,
Winding across wide water, without sound,
Stilled for the passing of her dreaming feet
Over the seas, to silent Palestine,
Dominion of the blood and sepulchre.

From *Sunday Morning* by Wallace Stevens (1915)★

She haunts my memory. There she sits, sipping her coffee with the citric tang of orange on her lips. A tame cockatoo struts about the carpet. Her silk dressing gown and the lateness of the morning tell us of her liberation from Sabbath duty, but, as the poem says, she still feels 'the dark encroachment of that old catastrophe', the ancient sacrifice of Christ in Palestine. 'Complacencies of the Peignoir' have almost dissipated her former belief, but not entirely. Doubt lingers at the margin. Habits of faith still encroach upon her Sunday morning.

I first heard her wistful yearning – 'the need for some imperishable bliss' – years ago, when I was at school. We were reading a selection of modern American verse, introduced to us by Roger Lockyer. He was one of those teachers who opened our eyes to the ambiguities of life. I still have the paperback edition of Geoffrey Moore's selection on my bookshelf with my name and the date, 1955, written on the cover.

Complacencies of the Peignoir, Roger quoted as we met recently for lunch. It was the first time we had met in sixty years. It was my decision to do so, prompted by a report in the papers: he and his partner, Percy Steven, had been among the first gay couples to be married under the new law, and, to their embarrassment, they received considerable attention in the press.

After such a long time, it was probable that he would not remember me. There must have been so many other former school pupils and university students whom he had taught during those years. As it happened, our meeting was a great success and marked the birth, and rebirth, of a friendship that the four of us were able to celebrate with regular lunches at Galvin's and at the Orrery in Marylebone, until his death in 2017. He was nearly ninety, but for us it felt too soon. For his partner Percy, it was a disaster.

Roger was one of John Dancy's best gifts to Lancing. He arrived, it seemed, straight from Cambridge, and, although he may have had another post before coming to us, he carried with him the freshness, enthusiasm and aesthetic awareness of a new age. For us he was a one-man Renaissance. He became head of history, and conducted seminars in his sitting room, treating us with great courtesy as undergraduates. Although we were studying the Tudors and Stuarts, discussion was not restricted. The latest play by Becket or novel by the then almost unknown Iris Murdoch, the furniture of the Brighton Pavilion, Inigo Jones's design for King James's Banqueting House or the best way of percolating coffee would be topics that would slip graciously and excitingly in and out of our conversation during his tutorials. In our English lessons he introduced us to the excitements of modern verse. He taught us to connect, and, I suppose, to grow up.

I cannot recall now why Roger should have quoted Wallace Stevens's poem. In a letter, he later wrote 'I am one of that large number of people who, while they have not been blessed with the gift of faith, care deeply for the Church of England.' I sensed that he, like the woman in the poem, was nostalgic for a faith he no longer possessed. But, for him, there was so much to enjoy in a life unencumbered by religion.

> Shall she not find in comforts of the sun,
> In pungent fruit and bright, green wings, or else
> In any balm or beauty of the earth,
> Things to be cherished like the thought of heaven?

Roger, I guess, must have found with his beloved partner 'comforts of the sun' and a share of 'things to be cherished like the thought of heaven'. Among those comforts, he would have counted their wide circle of friends who had gathered a year earlier at the Orrery to celebrate their golden jubilee; their regular visits to the theatre, too, would have played an important part; summers in their house in France and great vintages they had known, now recalled as they pored over the wine list and made their choice; and their delight in good food, informed by extensive culinary knowledge, which included the recipe for George I's Christmas pudding.

But I wonder if he shared with the woman in the poem, and with all of us for that matter, the wistful yearning for something more:

> She says, "But in contentment I still feel
> The need of some imperishable bliss."

To which the narrator's voice replies to her, as it does to us:

Death is the mother of beauty; hence from her,
Alone, shall come fulfilment to our dreams
And our desires.

And is the poet not right? Death is like the conclusion of a sonata, which gives form and meaning to what has gone before. Music without end would be sound without purpose; its beauty immeasurably damaged. 'Death is the mother of beauty.' Life without end would be intolerable. Mortality must be preferable to the burden of endless existence.

Roger has died. I count it one of life's great gifts that I knew him and learnt so much from him. At ninety death was inevitable and, for his many friends, it was a quiet conclusion to a life; an affirmation, not a denial. For his beloved partner, it has been and is an unimaginable loss.

*Extracts from *Sunday Morning* (Wallace Stevens 1879-1955) are printed by permission of Messrs Faber and Faber.

IS THERE A LIMIT TO OUR COMPASSION?

Nancy Mitford, in her novel *The Pursuit of Love*, describes young Linda as having an unlimited capacity for compassion. As a child, she spent much of her time weeping over the real or imagined disasters that afflicted the numerous family pets. So sensitive was she that books like *Black Beauty* had to be removed from the nursery. Her compassion for the suffering of helpless victims extended also to inanimate objects. One of her sisters composed this rhyme:

> *A little houseless match*
> *It has no roof, no thatch,*
> *It lies alone, it makes no moan,*
> *That little houseless match.*

This never failed to induce floods of tears, especially when chanted by her sisters in a low lugubrious monotone. At times they only had to glance at a matchbox on the table to dissolve her into helpless grief.

There is something about that induced compassion that calls to mind the pity we are asked to feel every day for the sufferings of the world. Our withers are wrung each time we switch on the news. Every day brings its disaster and invokes our compassion – until, that is, it is replaced by another catastrophe, then another and then another. Hurricanes in the Caribbean; forced migration of people in Burma; cholera in Yemen; refugees drowning in the Mediterranean; the slaughter by a lone gunman of civilians in a shopping mall, in a church or in a school; murder by truck; murder by bomb; disfigurement by acid; trafficking of women; abuse of children; a tower-block inferno in London; civil war in Sudan; atrocities in Syria; anarchy in Libya: these are just some of the current disasters of 2017. As the TV news bulletins bring us continuous accounts of catastrophe, we are bewildered how to react proportionately.

We simply cannot make an adequate response to every disaster that confronts us on our smartphone, TV or radio. And yet the skills of reporter and camera crew, often exercised in situations of great personal danger to themselves, are deployed precisely with that end in mind: not just to inform us, but to wring the last drop of pity from our hearts, and to go on doing so, day after day after day, on the assumption that our compassion is limitless.

That is why we are confronted by the weeping father holding his dead child, the twisted wreckage of a house after a tornado, the bandaged leg of an amputee, the mudslide that has just crushed and drowned a village, a bed hanging from a second storey, a child's trainer abandoned in the playground after a school massacre, and the desperate struggles of refugees drowning in the sea when their overcrowded boat has just capsized before our eyes. It does not help that the TV announcer introduces the footage with the warning that we may find some of the scenes disturbing. Of course we will! Why tell us in advance, if not to whet our appetite for more and more horrors for which to weep our tears or stoke our rage?

This is not to criticise our reporters and photographers, who do a courageous and honest job of telling the truth. Whether the broadcasters, with their eye on viewers' ratings, are innocent of the charge of cynical manipulation of the images provided by reporters is less clear.

What, then, distinguishes a legitimate call upon our compassion from a gratuitously lurid display to feed our voyeuristic appetite? Where to draw the line must be decided by the individual viewer's conscience, but that there is a distinction to be made should be publicly acknowledged by the programme makers of our media.

In an area in which it is unwise to make simplistic pronouncements, it does seem that the media, and in particular TV producers, need to be much more disciplined in the airtime they devote to disasters, and the quantity and the nature of the visual detail of suffering that they broadcast, if, that is, they are to be taken seriously in their claim to be responsible reporters of information and not just sensationalist entertainers. They could start by examining their motives for repeating up to three times within a single news programme the same harrowing footage of human suffering and violent death – first in the headline, then in the main story and, finally, in the closing summary.

What is the Christian response? We should start, as always, with Jesus himself and his own response to the suffering he encountered. His ministry of healing and compassion was not general. It was local and it was restricted. For every leper he cleansed, he must have known that there were hundreds in Galilee whom he did not; for every blind man he cured, there were scores he did not. His compassion was directed to the individual in front of him, and arose from a real and personal encounter. That should teach us something about the level and nature of our own response.

There is, of course, an obligation upon us to make a general response to the world's suffering. This we can do, for example, by a recurring banker's order to one of the general charities, such as the Disasters Emergency Committee or Christian Aid. Our regular giving, in that case, will be measured by a dispassionate assessment of how much of our disposable income we should be giving away. To be effective, this response should be rational and certainly should not need to be artificially pumped up by spasmodic appeals to our vulnerable feelings.

There is, however, a deeper response that Christians are called to make. When we pray for someone who is in 'trouble, sorrow, need or sickness', we are carrying that person to the foot of the Cross, to which Christ draws us all for his healing compassion. When Christ spoke those words – 'I, when I am lifted up from the earth will draw all people to myself' – he was calling us to share his own suffering; to be identified (compassionate) with his dying and rising again. Our prayer is not that we should be spared the pain, but that by his grace we can be transformed by it and not be defeated. That is a hard lesson to learn, and, in the eyes of an unbelieving world, it appears to make little sense. But that is what Christian compassion is: suffering and ultimately dying with Christ.

LONDON 7/7

(From a sermon preached at St Mary's Church, Worplesdon, 17th July 2005. During the previous fortnight, on Thursday 7th July, terrorists had bombed London, killing more than fifty people and injuring seven hundred; on Sunday 10th July the nation had celebrated the sixtieth anniversary of the end of World War II in May 1945; and on Thursday 14th July, at noon, two minutes' silence had been observed in memory of the victims of the bombing on the 7th)

Four powerful images appeared on our TV screens during the last two weeks.

First, the face of a young woman desperately searching for her fiancé a day after the London bombs. 'Have you seen him?' she kept asking passers-by, holding up a photograph. A few days later cameras picked her up again, still asking the same question, 'Have you seen him?' Visible to us all was her bewilderment and fear of the dreadful truth.

Then there was the image of another woman, a survivor of one of the bombs, haunted now by the guilt of having escaped when others hadn't. She told a reporter how, finding a way through the tangled wreckage of the underground train she had been travelling in, she had managed to scramble through to safety. But behind her she heard the groans and screams of those now beyond all help. 'Will they forgive me?' she sobbed and the reporter, suddenly overcome, shielded the woman from the camera's intrusive stare.

The third image was of the Lancaster bomber on the Sunday releasing thousands of red poppies over the crowds in the Mall as they commemorated the sixtieth anniversary of the end of World War II. The cloud of petals fluttered down like gentle healing rain; a beautiful sight in contrast to the damaged bodies and broken hearts of war. From violence and trauma to peace and reconciliation.

Then, on the Thursday in the week following the bombing, the people of London kept a silence at noon. They came out of their offices to stand together on the pavement. The shops fell silent. Pedestrians stood still. The buses pulled into the kerb. The traffic stopped. And, alone in the forecourt of that most sombre and overpowering building, Buckingham Palace, stood a small, solitary figure: the Queen.

It was a time for quiet reflection and for the dignity of sorrow; not a time for anger or recrimination. After the terror, a greater vision was needed. After the suffering, a hint of healing. After the tragedy can come a new hope.

The writer of the Book of Wisdom lived in the first century BC. He was a Jew living in Alexandria. He knew all about the violence of persecution. His response was gentle. He prayed to God in these words:

Although you are sovereign in strength, you judge with mildness and with forbearance you govern us… You have taught your people that the righteous must be kind and you have filled your children with good hope.

Wisdom 12:18,19

And, a century later, St Paul, another victim of violence who later faced martyrdom, wrote that out of his suffering came a greater vision of hope; a vision that we must today make our own:

I am convinced that neither death, nor life, nor angels, nor rulers, nor things present, nor things to come, nor powers, nor height, nor depth, nor anything else in all creation, will be able to separate us from the love of God in Christ Jesus.

Romans 8:38–39

A BYE-DAY WITH THE LOCAL HUNT

The new master came to us with the reputation for being a hard man. Comparisons were drawn with the legendary Master of the Galway Blazers – a man who had contained deep within him a seething volcanic fury of such violence that his huge turnip head had threatened in moments of stress to fly from his shoulders with a deafening report and a rush of flame. When one day the inevitable occurred, the explosion was heard three fields away. When they reached the spot, all that remained of him was the brim of his hat, hanging from a tree, and a pair of smoking boots. Or so they said.

Our new master was of that ilk.

My moment of glory came on a mid-week bye-day. The usual Saturday crowd was missing. Absent too were the saboteurs. There were present only half a dozen or so local farmers, the butcher from a neighbouring village, a retired schoolmaster, the Dunkerley girls (it was school half-term) and that formidable octogenarian, Biddy Blomfield. Rouged like a trollop and whiskered like a grenadier, she was a sight to strike terror into the boldest heart. She claimed never to have missed a day's hunting in the past twenty-five seasons.

As she passed me at the meet, my horse began to play up with a succession of short bucks. All very humiliating. It makes you look such a fool. In my confusion, I found myself slipping into the role of John Jorrocks. Surtees was at that time my favourite reading.

'Hold still,' I bellowed, as my mount began to caper on the spot. 'Stand, I say, you hugly beast! *Stand, you pig, you!* I'll larrup yer flanks, yer old nag.'

'Well, *really*,' said Miss Blomfield. 'Who the devil are you?'

I tried to explain the mistake, but before I could do so, my horse careered backwards into the path of the schoolmaster.

'*Look out, you fool*,' he shouted. I was shocked by the force of his language – such a gentle-looking man, too.

It was not a good start, though it could have been worse. At least I had managed to keep at a distance from the master. Hounds drew first at Turner's Roughs, and I was enjoying a moment of solitude, having decided for everyone's safety to remain away from the rest of the field.

It was one of those glorious, sparkling winter days, the very best for hounds. As I sat listening to the distant noises from the copse and waiting for the fox to break cover, I pondered the beauty of the landscape, 'plotted and pieced – fold, fallow and plough.'

Suddenly, there was an appalling commotion close by. The side of the wood nearest to me burst outwards with an explosion of twigs and foliage, as the master and his mount hurtled from the trees, his eyes glaring and his face empurpled with passion. He shouted at me:

'WHARROOBORLABARRFF?'

'I'm sorry,' I replied, my mouth dry with fear. 'I didn't quite catch—'

'ISAIDWHARROOBORLABARRFF. *BARRFF?*'

He came towards me at a canter. I believed he meant to strike me. As he drew closer, I could see his protruding eyes and gobbling rage. I foresaw it all: the terrible explosion, the searing pain, the smoking boots.

Then I looked beyond him, and saw what no one else could see. Concealed from everyone's view by a dip in the ground, a large dog fox was loping casually right to left, away from Turner's Roughs towards a sixteen-acre ploughed field.

By some half-forgotten instinct, and without a thought for safety or decorum, I stood up in my stirrups, flung out my arm in the direction of the fox and let fly an ear-splitting holler, which could have been heard in the next county. Surtees would have been proud – though not Archbishop Harcourt, who told Sidney Smith that he did not mind his clergy hunting, so long as they did not shout.

It was the work of a moment, but enough to earn myself the spurious character of a *hunting parson*. As the master wheeled his horse and called up his hounds – as he set them to the line – as the rest of the field cantered over towards me, and then surged after the hounds in what was to be the start of a five-mile point, the longest of the season – I knew that I had secured my reputation.

'Nice one,' wheezed the butcher, as he lumbered past on his wall-eyed cob. 'Splendid... splendid,' acknowledged the schoolmaster, with a gracious inclination of his head, amounting almost to a benediction. After them came the Dunkerley girls, and behind them, as chaperone, their father's farm manager. He was having a tough job keeping up with his young charges. Then, just as I thought it safe to tag along, Miss Blomfield charged past on her corn-fed stallion in a whirl of reins and blasphemy.

Recollection of the details of that run is blurred: the fences we hurdled, the hedges we jumped, the ditches we leapt, the lanes we hurtled down, the gateways we bundled through, the farmsteads we came upon suddenly and then as suddenly left, the pasture we traversed and the plough we skirted, the geese we scattered, the dogs we woke and the villages we astounded. But, if memory of the individual elements is confused, the overall impression is distinct enough: I was beside myself, intoxicated by a madness that made me laugh and shout.

Later, as I soaked in a long, hot bath, drinking a second mug of steaming tea laced with a restorative slug of Jameson's, I relived my hour of glory. It was then that I decided to give it all up. I knew that I would never again experience such exhilaration. Such a glorious and unforgettable gallop comes only once in a lifetime. It was prudent, I considered, to get out now, when I was, as it were, ahead of the field.

I never hunted again.

JACOB'S LADDER

Stairs figure prominently in dreams. They always have done. Ever since the dawn of recorded time, men and women have dreamt of climbing a stairway to heaven. Some of the earliest surviving stairways are those built on the outside of Aztec pyramids, which the sun-worshipping priests would climb to offer their grisly sacrifices.

In the ancient story of the Tower of Babel there are echoes of the Mesopotamian ziggurats, pyramidal buildings by whose stairways the Sumerian priests made their liturgical ascent to heaven – an attempt that, in the Hebrew version, was confounded by Yahweh so that he might teach us arrogant mortals a lesson.

In one of their most exacting dance sequences, Fred Astaire and Ginger Rogers danced up a double flight of stairs. The movement begins in a muted way; the romance between the characters having cooled somewhat because of a misunderstanding. Then, as they dance, at first hesitantly, but with growing confidence, the music and choreography tell that love has been recaptured. They glide and spin and pirouette, as exhilaration takes hold and the tempo of the music accelerates. Then, at last, they dance up the double stairway – he on the left flight, she on the right. They meet at the top and their love is sealed in a sequence of ecstatic spins.

'Heaven, I'm in heaven,' they might well have sung at the top of those stairs, though that was on another occasion and in a different film.

Jacob spoke of heaven too. In the book of Genesis (28:10–17), we are told that he had broken his journey to spend the night on the hillside. There he dreamt of a different stairway, one that he could not climb. It was a ladder stretching from earth to heaven, on which angels were moving up and down. 'Surely, the Lord is in this place, and I did not know it,' he said when he awoke. 'This is none other than the house of God, and this is the gate of heaven.'

He was a down-to-earth sort of man, not given to flights of fancy, at least not during his waking hours. He was an ambitious striver, shrewd and devious in his dealings. Even so, he knew the importance of his dream. Here was evidence that the world he inhabited and knew so well – a world of tribal feuds, intrigue and cheating – was linked to a higher and nobler realm and that he, rogue that he was, had been given a glimpse of heaven and an assurance of that link.

But – and here is the point – his eyes were fixed upon the foot of the ladder, not the top. 'The Lord is in this place,' he said, looking at the hillside where he stood, 'And I did not know it. This is none other than the house of God' and then, looking at the harsh, rock-strewn landscape, he added, 'This is the gate of heaven'.

The ladder had its top in the clouds, but its feet, like Jacob's, were firmly planted on the ground.

Like Jacob, we are down-to-earth people, caught up in the struggles of an imperfect world and, like Jacob not above a little bit of sharp practice to get our way. Like him we need our ladder, a stairway that links our disordered and fractured world to heaven. We need not only sacred places like church or synagogue, mosque or temple, but hidden moments and silences in our lives to which we can point and say, 'Surely, the Lord is in this place, and I knew it not. This is none other than the house of God, and this is the gate of heaven.'

THE SONGBIRDS OF ISTANBUL

Every Friday afternoon the ladies of the sultan's harem would make their weekly outing to the shops on the *Grande Rue de Pera*. Scores of royal carriages, ornamented with silver rails and lanterns, would set off from the Dolmabahçe Palace on the shores of the Bosphorus. In each carriage were four or five veiled ladies, on the box was a coachman in the blue-and-gold imperial livery and, seated next to him in black frock coat, a eunuch from the royal harem. It was customary for the male staff of the British embassy located in that quarter of Constantinople, where my grandfather worked, to stay tactfully indoors during those afternoons.

The *Grande Rue*, known then as 'The Paris of the East', was the venue for art galleries, pastry cooks, chocolatiers, French milliners and dress shops containing the latest Parisian gowns. Among these luxuries the ladies were able, fleetingly, to indulge themselves, and not least in the sweetshop of the imperial confectioner Haçi Bekir, whose loucoums were, as we would now say, something to die for.

Also on sale were songbirds in little golden cages. These pretty creatures were of special appeal to the prisoners of the Seraglio, whose fancy it was to buy them and release them to the freedom of the open sky, not observing the watchful hawks that circled in the skies above the city, especially on a Friday afternoon.

In summer, by way of another diversion, the ladies would enjoy excursions to 'The Sweet Waters of Europe', a pleasaunce of flower-strewn meadows and pretty streams. There they would spread their rugs to picnic and watch the families sitting on the grass with their children. They would laugh at the young men as they ran races and showed off on their horses.

Years later, the last sultan of the Ottoman Empire was deposed and the ladies of the royal harem were dispersed. The government sent messages throughout the Ottoman territories, calling for the next-of-kin to claim their lost relations. Two hundred and thirteen pampered ladies were sent back to their villages.

'Would that we had died by the hand of the Lord in Egypt when we sat by the fleshpots and when we did eat bread to the full.' Some of the harem had come from Christian families and would have been familiar with the plight of the Israelites when Moses liberated them from Pharaoh's bondage. 'And not only bread,' they would have thought, 'Not only did we eat bread to the full, but baklava, too, and loucoum and grapes and rose-scented cordials as we listened to music at night in the marble halls of the sultan's court.'

'Freedom,' they must have thought as they lived out their lives in rural poverty, 'Who wants freedom?'

They were the lucky ones. At least they had relations to come and take them to their homes. But for the others who were left behind, no one ever came.

OLD TOBY PLANS HIS FUNERAL

'And so, about this funeral of mine…'

Toby returned to what had become a favourite subject. In recent months he had taken to his bed, allowing the nurses in his care home to wash him and turn him and gently cajole him. In response, he would make roguish comments and be told not to be a naughty boy. How the old fellow had mellowed, I thought, and wondered if I would be so patient when my time came.

'*Si jeunesse savait*' he would murmur at one of the younger staff, and then with a sigh, '*Si vieillaise pouvait* Ah well, all passion spent. What was I saying?'

'Your funeral, Toby'

'Ah, yes, about this funeral of mine. I want none of your mealy-mouthed cant. None of that mawkish drivel that nowadays passes for a funeral. Death deserves better. I must have solemnity. *Gravitas*. The French are right, you know: *pompes funèbres*. Pomp – that's the thing. Pomp. Let there be muffled drums, horses with black plumes. My hunter, Caliph, led behind the coffin, with boots reversed in the stirrups. Then the carriages – ah, yes, the carriages – and all my women veiled in deep mourning. I can see them now…'

His voice trailed away as he considered with lugubrious pleasure the prospect of his own forthcoming obsequies. Increasingly these days, there sounded in his conversation a valedictory note. He had always been able to paint reality in noble colours, and who could blame him if to do so he sometimes leant too much upon the power of his own imagination. For Toby, fantasy and reality dovetailed together, but sometimes they overlapped, with one obscuring the other.

Ever since I had known him it had been his private pleasure to play out little dramas by which to enliven what he felt was the banality of existence. For example, a few years earlier, he had chosen to invent a wholly fictitious scenario with which to enact his role as church treasurer – heaven knows, not the most obvious setting for any kind of original screenplay. I came upon this by accident when I surprised him one Monday morning as he was counting up the Sunday collections.

Between him and his wife there lay on the kitchen table his service revolver, fully loaded, as I discovered when he later emptied the cartridges on to the table. 'Can't be too careful,' he said as he put the gun away, 'Never know, these days.' It pleased him to heighten the risk of burglary, introducing an element of danger into the otherwise mundane narrative of life.

The point of these little enactments was that they were rarely disclosed, but remained for his own private entertainment. The players were kept unaware of the parts they had been given, but I would know that something was up when I saw his shoulders shaking in silent mirth. On one occasion, quite early in my time in the parish, he told me that he could only survive the *longueurs* of meetings of the parochial church council by secretly casting his fellow members as characters from the novels of Charles Dickens and R S Surtees. Soapy Sponge, Mr Jawleyford, Mrs Jellyby, Uriah Heap and, inevitably, Mr Micawber had all at one time or another taken part in discussions about such bitterly contested topics as the purchase of new hymn books or the disposal of a redundant pew.

'And the music,' he said, returning to the subject, 'I want the choir to sing *Thou Knowest, Lord, the Secrets of Our Hearts.* Purcell at his best, don't you think? And then, as they carry me out,' he spoke more eagerly as he warmed to his subject, 'as the cortège moves slowly down the nave to the great west doors, the choir will be singing the Morley setting of the Nunc Dimittis. *Lord, now lettest thou thy servant depart in peace.* I can hear it now. Wonderful, wonderful.'

'And hymns?' I asked, after a pause.

'Do we have to?'

'It is usual.'

'Oh well, if we have to. But not *Jerusalem.* Dreadful nonsense. Poor old Blake. You know he went completely bonkers. Used to take his clothes off in the garden and read Milton. Persuaded Mrs Blake to do so, too.'

In the event, it was just as Toby had wished. No eulogy. No jokes. Death was acknowledged in all its mystery and solemnity in the words of the Burial Office of the *Book of Common Prayer.* The choir did him proud with Purcell, as did the large congregation with *Immortal, Invisible, God only Wise.*

To all life thou givest, to both great and small;
In all life thou livest, the true life of all;
We blossom and flourish as leaves on the tree
And wither and perish, but nought changeth thee.

In the event, we were not able to provide a horse-drawn hearse, nor was Caliph available – he had been long since gathered into the great paddock in the skies, no doubt waiting patiently there for his master to take him out for a brisk hack, just like in the old days.

PRISON VISIT

We were visiting prison. David Hypher, in his official capacity as High Sheriff, had asked me, as one of his chaplains, to accompany him. It is one of the High Sheriff's duties to visit all the prisons in his county. So there we were, standing in a cell talking to its occupant, Paul (not his real name). There were five of us: a senior prison officer, David, his wife Pam (our chauffeur for the day, as David was not able to drive), Paul and me.

As prison cells go, it was reasonably comfortable: it was furnished with bed, table, chair, cupboard, bookshelf and TV. To these bare necessities Paul had added photographs of his wife and children. We were told not to ask or discuss the reason why he was in prison, but he was keen to tell us all the same. Up until his conviction his life, he said, was a mess – heroin had been just one of the causes, though he admitted that it was the chief.

During his time in prison he had undertaken an enhanced thinking course. This, he said, had taught him to think positively about life and, most importantly, about himself. He had learnt to correct the low self-esteem that, he said, was a cause of his bad behaviour. He had also attended a training course on industrial cleaning – how to clean a variety of surfaces, fabrics and furnishings. With pride he showed us the six NVQ (City and Guilds) certificates he had gained during his time in prison. He had been equipped with qualifications and so, when he was released into the world, he would have a chance to start again.

As he was talking, I looked at the pictures of his family and wondered how it would all turn out.

An hour later, David, Pam and I were talking to one of the deputy governors. She was sharp, smart and young. Surely, I thought, the optimism of youth would be as yet untarnished by the weary cynicism of the professional gaoler. We repeated Paul's story. Here was success; here was an example of what an enlightened prison regime could achieve.

'What was his name?' she asked. We told her. 'Oh, him. Yes, he's done pretty well. He'll be out in a few weeks. Then…' She stopped.

'Then?' we said.

'Then, he'll be back. He'll leave here, go back home, meet up with his old mates, and within a couple of months – well, you know how it is.'

She had seen it all. She knew too much. She and Paul were both victims of society's tragic failure, for which, I suppose, we must all bear some blame.

SAVE THE CHILDREN

(From an article published in the *Church Times*,
17th December 2004)

It is a pity there was no colour photography when Eglantine Jebb was young. We can only guess at the red-gold hair and blue eyes. Even so, what we have in black and white is the picture of a beautiful young woman.

Her beauty was not the only thing that strangers saw; they remembered something else. They noticed a diffidence behind the self-assurance. Some sensed a detachment; not quite aloofness, more a discomfort. The more perceptive saw deeper: her Oxford tutor feared that the girl – who as a teenager had ridden fearlessly to hounds, climbed trees, boated in the summer, skated in the winter and raised from her brothers and sisters a regiment of light cavalry – might yet turn her back upon the world.

She was loved by her fellow undergraduates, but not by all. She entered fully into the life of the university – lectures, debating, punting, hockey and dancing through the night at the New College Ball. But some were wary, especially those whom she called 'the dress-and-tea-party set'.

The clouds of depression gathered (years later a thyroid condition was diagnosed). She believed that she had failed as a schoolteacher. Nothing could dispel her self-doubt, not even the urchins that clamoured daily at her lodgings for the favour of walking with her to school.

Then she had the spiritual experience that changed her life:

In my trouble there came to me the face of Christ... Above my class hung a cheap print of His thorn-crowned head. I saw an expression of unspeakable suffering, but suffering which was conquered by resignation... Then I knew what I had never known before, how we need God in Christ, as well as God the Father. Then in the moment of my sorrow I found a happiness which, please God, shall light my life and make my lips speak praise till death.

Liberated, she was able to fight for social justice on many fronts. Her report on poverty in Cambridge broke new ground. She wrote the following in 1906:

The wretchedness of the urban poor can no longer be taken for granted, or their circumstances regarded as unalterable. We have created [those conditions] ourselves and are responsible for combating them.

In 1919, while the country clamoured for revenge against the defeated Germans, she campaigned on behalf of the starving children of Central Europe, victims of Britain's blockade of a broken people. From this was born the Save the Children Fund.

She had twice been disappointed in love. 'I feel now as if I have been for years on a desert island, straining my eyes for a ship that does not come', she wrote to a friend. Then, in her journal, 'I have one thing left; I have some work to do.'

PROCESSIONS

(From a sermon preached in Guildford Cathedral
on Quinquagesima Sunday, 1989)

Processions can be splendid occasions; they can also be disasters. Briefly, a procession is a liturgical device by which the church enacts themes of pilgrimage and celebration that are basic to the Gospel. It is not just a way of moving a body of people from one part of the building to another. The movement itself is an act of worship.

Well, that's the theory. But, as every cathedral precentor knows, congregational processions can go spectacularly wrong. As a young country parson, I once staged a Palm Sunday procession round the outside of the parish church. It was the first recorded procession in that church since the Reformation, when such things had been banned. After an interval of four hundred years it was important to get it right.

The organist and I worked out the route. The congregation, led by the choir, were to leave by the south door, process halfway round the outside of the church and re-enter by the north door. We walked the course with the crucifer, acolytes and choir. We timed the distance and calculated the number of verses of *All Glory, Laud and Honour* that we would need.

The day came. The organist struck up, and the long column of choir and people began to move with great dignity down the nave and out into the churchyard. All went well until the head of the procession re-entered by the north door. What happened next was what every pageant-master fears most, more even than a thunderstorm. The head of the procession collided with the tail. The whole column ground to a standstill. You will appreciate that there is no known liturgical manoeuvre by which you can release such a deadlock with dignity.

Our mistake, apart from the obvious lack of traffic control, was that we were taking it all much too seriously. We were far too solemn and pious, and so what might have been a slight hitch became a catastrophe.

There is a world of difference between a procession of robed choir and clergy, and one in which the congregation is invited to take part. Choir and clergy are required to behave in a formal manner. On the whole, members of the cathedral congregation do not wish the clergy and choir to pass through their midst with nods and winks of recognition. At most, the bishop or dean, or, in their absence, the canon-in-residence, might allow to pass momentarily across his features the shadow of a smile such as you would expect to see on the face of mildly amused archangel. An impish grin or thumbs-up gesture would be considered an unwarrantable intrusion.

But congregational processions are altogether more relaxed. They have to be. Once you get a congregation on the hoof, all sorts of interesting things begin to happen. An informality, an untidiness, enters the liturgy. And, with it a touch of levity; a hint, almost, of carnival. We should not be afraid of that. Solemnity in worship can be edged with levity, without loss of reverence. And, anyway, liturgy by its very nature forever teeters on the brink of farce: I once snagged my foot in an obstacle that had been left on the floor beside one of the pews. Being unable to disentangle my foot (I was robed and carrying a large processional candlestick, and so both hands were full) I had no choice but to continue down the semi-darkened nave dragging the thing along, and occasionally shaking my foot in an attempt to get rid of it. As we turned at the west end and began to move in stately fashion round the back, before turning east up the side aisle, I became aware of a lady bearing down upon us from the opposite direction in an outflanking movement. 'My bag,' she said, 'Young man, you have my bag.' In a moment she deftly detached it from my foot, and I was able to continue on my way without let or hindrance.

There is another important thing that happens during a congregational procession. It springs from the very act of walking together. In human experience there can be no greater symbols of friendship than the shared meal and the shared walk. Our worship transmutes these ordinary activities into the Eucharist and the Procession.

It has not always been thus. There was a period in our church's history when the procession, the shared walk, fell out of use. After the Reformation, we became a sedentary church. We filled our churches with box pews, each with its door and high partitions. Impossible it was with such furniture to move out of our narrow enclosures. Our religion became a private matter.

Then, in the late Victorian period, we became once more a mobile church. Not only did choir and clergy take to perambulating the aisles of the church, but entire congregations could be seen on festivals processing through the streets of our greater cities such as Liverpool, Leeds, Manchester, Portsmouth and London.

Bishops found themselves, sometimes to their alarm, caught up in this new enthusiasm. Not all of them were convinced that it was compatible with episcopal dignity. Dr Gilbert of Chichester compromised by following the robed clergy in a hansom cab. When the choir, who were singing Psalm 150, reached the final verse, the bishop, with impeccable timing, ordered the cab driver to stop, and stepped down in time for the *Gloria Patri*.

Since those days, the clergy have become less hesitant. The

sight of bishops walking with their people is commonplace. It is, you might think, a small thing and hardly worth noticing, but it is a sign of grace that we who were once so sedentary have taken to our feet. As a Church we are called to move onwards, sometimes reluctantly, and to step beyond the safe enclosure of our own traditions. And in doing so (who knows?) we might find ourselves falling in with unfamiliar company, as did those two disciples one Sunday evening so many years ago on their walk home to Emmaus.

AN OLD-FASHIONED SCHOOLMASTER

Richard Busby (1606–1695)

(First published in the *Church Times*, April 2013)

Richard Busby, born in 1606, was educated at Westminster School and Christ Church, Oxford, where he stayed as tutor for ten years. In 1638 he was appointed headmaster of Westminster, where he remained in post until his death nearly sixty years later. He was ordained in 1639. He was admired by his former students as the greatest teacher of his age and was feared in equal measure as its most vigorous disciplinarian. Among his pupils were Christopher Wren, John Locke and John Dryden.

When asked how he managed to preserve his school during the turbulence of the seventeenth century, Busby said, 'The fathers rule the country, the mothers rule the fathers, the boys rule their mothers, and I rule the boys.' The story, probably apocryphal, is a fair assessment of the school's proximity to the seat of power: school and Parliament were neighbours.

That the school prayed for King Charles I on the morning of his execution was not held against it. Parliament protected its endowments from sequestration under the Root and Branch Act for the abolition of ecclesiastical corporations. The headmaster was careful not to identify the school with the current regime. The royalist Sackvilles sent their sons there and so did the Parliamentarian Russells.

His predecessor, the Reverend Lambert Osbaldston, had been deprived and put in the pillory for calling Archbishop Laud 'a little meddling hocus pocus'. Busby was more prudent, though he did not always conceal his views. 'You were of another faith when you were under me,' he said when he met a former pupil who had converted to Rome. 'How dared you change it?' 'The Lord had need of me,' was the reply. Busby's response was, 'I never knew the Lord had need of anything but once, and then it was an ass.'

He was a *Prayer Book* man, and despised the *Directory for Public Worship*, which had replaced the *Book of Common Prayer*. He held clandestine services according to the proscribed rite of the *Book of Common Prayer* in his house, which a former pupil and future bishop, Edward Wetenhall, described as 'a more regular church than most we had publicly'.

Philip Henry, a leading dissenter, recalled with gratitude not only his headmaster's severity, but also 'the solemn preparation for the Communion then observed'. His piety was mentioned, too, by Anthony à Wood, the usually scabrous Oxford antiquary. Busby, he said, was 'a person eminent and exemplary for piety and justice, an encourager of virtuous and forward youth, of great learning and hospitality [who had] educated more youths that were afterwards eminent in the Church and State than any master of his time.'

John Evelyn, the diarist, was present as the pupils competed for election to the universities. 'I heard and saw such exercises… in Latin, Greek, Hebrew and Arabic… as wonderfully astonished me in such youths… some of them not above twelve or thirteen years of age.'

Pupils, especially those who boarded at the headmaster's house, were exposed to the breadth of his enquiring mind and conversation. According to Aubrey, Robert Hooke, inventor of the microscope, learnt the organ, was 'very mechanical' and invented 'thirty several ways of flying' during his time as a boarder.

Busby claimed to have birched sixteen future bishops; a modest score, considering his innings of nearly sixty years.

During his lifetime, and by his will, he disposed of considerable wealth in support of debtors, impoverished clergy, lectureships and parish libraries. To this day trustees manage his several benefactions.

Posthumous busts, based upon his death mask, show a peevish aspect. By contrast, his portrait in Christ Church hall – a later version hangs in the National Portrait Gallery – depicts humour and strength. His hat says much. His account books reveal an extensive wardrobe, including an 'Indian gown' and a pair of hose in the 'Spanish fashion'. He also enjoyed wine and tobacco.

'Busby's genius for education', wrote Richard Steele in 1714, 'had as great an effect upon the age he lived in, as that of any ancient philosopher, without excepting one, had upon his contemporaries.'

He died on 5th April 1695; his grave and monument are in Westminster Abbey.

STANSTEAD AIRPORT

28th August 2006

Airports stand at the crossroads of a thousand private journeys. So many lives momentarily touch, pause, and then diverge to foreign lands and distant cities: Paris, Oslo, Frankfurt, Krakow, Prague, Tirana, Ljubljana and Istanbul. The flight-departures board carries the mind back to old migrations, along paths once taken by our distant forefathers – Saxons, Vikings, Franks, Poles, Magyars, Slavs, Jews and Turks – and now by us, their descendants, on voluntary, peaceful errands.

Such a concourse of people is gathered haphazardly, while outside the perimeter fence of the airfield's no man's land lies England with her little fields, hedgerows and villages, bearing names like Dunmow, Felsted, Pleshey, Butcher's Pasture and Takeley Street.

I had an hour to kill, and so did what I had never done before: I visited the airport chapel. I found there, pinned to the board, four prayer requests. The first, written in a sloping, continental hand, read:

Merci, Seigneur, pour ce voyage et l'accueil de Dace mon amie. Je te confie les personnes rencontrées et celles que je vais retrouver. Garde moi dans la fidelité à ton amour.
[Thank you, Lord, for my safe arrival and thank you, too, for my friend, Dace, and her hug of welcome. May God bless us all, the friends I shall meet again, and those whose friendship I had lost awhile, but will now renew. Keep us, Lord, trusting in your loving protection]

The second request asked 'Please pray for Hesse. He is one year old. He is very ill.' Who can tell what anguish the little boy's family must have been going through? Hear, Lord, this call for help from his father on his necessary but unwelcome business trip away from his home in Germany.

A third note, pencilled in capitals, cried out 'Pray for Palestine to be free.' During that summer of 2006, Ariel Sharon's wall of separation was still being extended, Hamas continued to strengthen its hold on Gaza and the West Bank, and peace looked further away than ever.

The fourth message read 'Please, Lord, bless me and my girlfriend. We love each other very much. Please may we never stop loving each other.' It was written in a round feminine hand. Was there in that prayer the fear that society's hostility might draw the lovers apart? Or, by God's grace, would they be able hold their course and learn like Shakespeare's lovers to 'look on tempests and be never shaken'?

And what of my prayer? As I listened to those voices, I was drawn into the intimacy of other people's lives: a group of friends, a sick child, an oppressed people and a loving couple. We were strangers to each other, but, at that moment in time and in the tiny enclosure of that airport chapel, we were brought together into his presence and enfolded in his love.

Silent acknowledgement was all my prayer and then, like them, I stepped back into the restless traffic of countless, intersecting lives, each with its private freight of joy and sorrow, anxiety and hope.

THE ALFRED JEWEL

(First published in the *Church Times*, 20th October 2006)

In 1693, after nearly a thousand years of legend, there came at last some tangible evidence: a jewel lay glinting on a rutted track not far from Athelney. It was made of gold and crystal, and enclosed a picture in cloisonné enamel of a seated figure, perhaps Christ. It bore an inscription in Saxon of '*AELFRED MEC HEHT GEWERCAN*' (Alfred had me made).

The jewel is thought to have once held a pointer, used to help in reading. When King Alfred sent to each of the bishops his own translation of Pope Gregory's manual for clergy, *Pastoral Care*, he wrote that he enclosed with every copy a jewelled pointer. After the strategy of war, he now turned to the arts of peace to reform the manners of his people and their clergy.

He did not neglect his defeated enemy, Guthrum. By the Treaty of Wedmore, the Danish king forswore the Norse gods and submitted to Christian baptism, with Alfred as godfather. For twelve days, victor and vanquished kept a feast.

Kingship required Alfred to be a lawgiver as well as a warrior. He inherited and modified the ancient Germanic codes of Offa and Ine. He looked also to the Bible and to Charlemagne for inspiration. And, as Charlemagne had done before, Alfred saw himself as descendant and servant of both imperial and papal Rome. He did not forget that, as an infant, he had been confirmed by Pope Leo IV in St Peter's and given the dignity of Roman Consul.

How great Alfred's scholarship was is uncertain. It was probably overstated by his friend and biographer, Asser. What is clear is that he was a keen learner. He kept a commonplace book (his *handboc*).

He assembled a group of scholars to work with him in translating Latin texts. Few of the secular clergy then understood Latin, and educational standards had sunk low. To reform the Church, he provided her with English translations of standard Latin texts. In his preface to Gregory's *Pastoral Care*, he gives us a picture of how he worked. He translated the Latin into English:

> *Sometimes word for word, sometimes sense for sense, as I learnt it from Plegmund my archbishop, and from Asser my bishop, and from Grimbold my mass-priest, and from John my mass-priest. After I had mastered it, I translated it into English as best I understood it and as I could most meaningfully render it.*

Alfred drew up a reading scheme for his clergy. As well as Gregory's handbook for clergy, he chose Bede's *Ecclesiastical History*, Orosius's *History Against the Pagans*, Boethius's *Consolation of Philosophy* and Augustine's *Soliloquies*, the last two translated by himself. It is in his own, rather free, translation ('sense for sense' rather than 'word for word') that we read his personal signature.

Behind the battles and the legends and the flattery, we get glimpses of the man. Shrewd, determined, brave, wary and pious. Harsh experience had left its mark. In his commentary on his translation of Psalm 2 (*Quare Fremuerunt Gentes* [Why do the heathen so furiously rage together?]), the once fugitive king in the Athelney marshes drew comfort from David and all his troubles.

As for that other story of the Athelney marshes – the burnt cakes – we have Archbishop Matthew Parker to thank for that. He added it, along with much else, to Asser's *Life* in 1574. The only surviving copy of Asser's biography was destroyed by fire in the eighteenth century.

The later tradition that presents him as Alfred the Great, founding father of Britain's maritime empire, derives from Thomas Arne's masque *Alfred* (1740) with its rousing chorus *Rule, Britannia*. By including his name in her calendar of saints, the Church has reclaimed his earlier fame: Alfred, the wisest of rulers and 'greatest treasure-giver of all kings' (Bishop Wulfsige of Sherborne).

Alfred's memorial is to be found, not so much in the unreliable written record or in later tradition but in the landscape of Wessex, the street plans of her ancient boroughs, the continuity of our oldest institution, the Church – and in a scholar's jewelled bookmark.

THE SOUND OF WORDS

The spoken word must have its own music, and never is this more important than in the words we use in worship. During the sixteenth century, when the Church of England was undergoing its first liturgical reformation, the official restrictions imposed upon church music were mitigated by the sound of Cranmer's liturgy, which contains within its cadences the music of the spoken word. Cranmer admitted that he had no ear for choral music, but he did have an ear for the sound of liturgical prose.

We must not suppose that in his 1549 *Book of Common Prayer* people heard the sound of sixteenth-century speech. That was not the case. Its rhythm was not at all the natural rhythm of spoken English. Cranmer's language in the prayers he composed – in most cases translations from the Latin collects of the pre-Reformation Church – was quite different from the vernacular of daily conversation. The language of the *Book of Common Prayer* was written for a different purpose. It was an artefact skilfully contrived to bear the repetition of public worship.

When Cranmer expressed himself in ordinary English, he did so in a quite shockingly coarse and jagged fashion. Nowhere is this more obvious than in his correspondence about the shortcomings of cathedral clergy. They were, he wrote, 'Loitering lubbers... who spent their time in much idleness, and their substance in superfluous belly cheer.' In those words we can hear the authentic sound of Tudor speech.

His genius was to create a distinct language, an artificial style of liturgical prose, which was so musical that it sounded natural. Take for example the Second Collect of Morning Prayer:

O God who art the author of peace and lover of concord, in knowledge of whom standeth our eternal life, whose service is perfect freedom: defend us thy humble servants in all assaults of our enemies; that we, surely trusting in thy defence, may not fear the power of any adversaries; through the might of Jesus Christ our Lord.

This prayer comes from the pre-Reformation monastic office of Lauds, which the monks sang at dawn, and derives ultimately from an eighth-century sacramentary. Throughout Charlemagne's empire, in Aachen, Tours and Lyon, half-awake in draughty abbeys, monks would have sung this prayer in Latin. Centuries later the monks of Winchester and Canterbury sang the same words: *'Deus auctor pacis et amator, quem nosse vivere: cui servire, regnare est.'*

And, centuries later still, Cranmer took those twelve words of terse Latin and gave us twenty-four words of graceful English. That was his skill. *'Amator'* became 'Lover of concord'. *'Quem nosse vivere'* became 'In knowledge of whom standeth our eternal life'. And *'cui servire, regnare est'* became 'whose service is perfect freedom'.

He understood that liturgical speech demands more words than simple prose, otherwise the mind cannot keep up with the sense. For the congregation to express public contrition it was not enough simply to say 'Sorry'. Instead, we learnt to recite the following:

Almighty God, Father of our Lord Jesus Christ, Maker of all things, Judge of all men; we acknowledge and bewail our manifold sins and wickedness, which we from time to time most grievously have committed, by thought, word and deed, against thy divine majesty, provoking most justly thy wrath and indignation against us…

The effect of this orotund style was not simply to express a penitence we might not feel, but to create in our hearts the penitence we ought to feel.

The language of *Common Worship* (2000) has its own music, too. For example, the Confession and Post-Communion prayers in the service of Holy Communion have a rhythm and directness that make them 'work' as liturgy when recited by the congregation at the Parish Eucharist. At first, some of us found them too spare, even abrupt, compared with what we had been accustomed to, but now, after nearly twenty years of use, most of us have learnt to value them not simply as 'fit for purpose' but as worthy of the affection that they deserve. This is true especially of the longer of the two Post-Communion prayers:

Father of all,
we give you thanks and praise,
that when we were still far off
you met us in your Son and brought us home.
Dying and living, he declared your love,
gave us grace, and opened the gate of glory.
May we who share Christ's body live his risen life;
we who drink his cup bring life to others;
we whom the Spirit lights give light to the world.
Keep us firm in the hope you have set before us,
so we and all your children shall be free,
and the whole earth live to praise your name;
through Christ our Lord.
Amen

SAY ONE FOR ME, VICAR

I was hurrying along the pavement to church, later than I should have been. A car went by and, as it passed, one of the passengers shouted through his open window, 'Say one for me, Vicar.' Clergy get used to joshing comments hurled at them out of passing cars. All part of the job, really. A small price to pay, but mildly irritating all the same.

In the vestry, the Eucharistic vestments awaited me – chasuble, stole and alb – all correctly folded and put one on top of the other in the order of vesting. Placed upon them was a note to remind me to read the banns of marriage ('If any of you know cause or just impediment why these two persons should not be joined together in Holy Matrimony, ye are to declare it.') and not to forget to call for volunteers to help next Saturday in the churchyard clear-up effort.

As a retired cleric, I am grateful for necessary reminders. There was a time when I could celebrate the Eucharist without all those little orange post-it notes stuck on the pages of the service book, and without which I would now be all at sea: 'Omit Gloria in Lent', 'Remind congregation to use alternative response in the intercessions', 'Turn to page 191 for Eucharistic Prayer C', 'Turn to page 309 for Proper Preface (Lent)', 'Go back to page 182 for post-communion prayers' or 'On first Sunday of month, replenish aumbry.' These days a priest has to be on his or her toes.

On this particular Sunday, I managed to conduct the service without any embarrassing hiatus or unexpected deviation from the script. Even the radio mic worked without mishap and, for once, the wire did not get into a tangle, as it sometimes does when it passes like a trailing vine beneath the folds of chasuble and alb to a concealed transmitter tucked into my trouser pocket.

There was only one unexpected interruption. We were just beginning the service when a police car, followed by an ambulance, went speeding along the road outside, sirens at full blast. But we were used to that. We carried on with the liturgy, enclosed in the 'God box', but aware of his world outside.

During the intercessions led by one of the congregation, my mind wandered back to the words, shouted at me from the passing car: 'Say one for me, Vicar.' 'Yes, mate,' I thought, 'that's just what I am doing. Saying one for you.' It was not kindly meant. It was just the sort of smug rejoinder that our Lord would have attributed to the Pharisee in the parable: 'Lord, I thank you that I am not as other people. I go to church on Sunday and pray for godless people, including young men in cars jeering as they speed by…'

In the hall after the service I found the woman whose banns I had read. Her fiancé had just come in from the churchyard, where he had been trying to find a signal for his mobile.

'Good news and bad news,' he said. 'I found a signal all right. Bad news is that the road just south of here has been closed. There's been a pile-up.'

I found out later that the driver and his passenger were both young men. One had been killed.

THE DEATH OF BENEDICT BISCOP

(From an article published in the *Church Times*,
19th January 2018)

'The past is a foreign country; they do things differently there.' L P Hartley's much quoted words at the beginning of his novel *The Go-Between* continue to resonate sixty-five years after they were written. Most of us would agree: the past *is* a foreign country, but there are times when we come within touching distance of its borders.

Weather can stir imagined memories of places we have never visited. And not only the climate but even the time of day. When Tennyson describes the island of the lotus eaters as a land 'in which it seemed always afternoon', we know exactly what he means. 'Afternoon': just the sound of those three syllables predisposes us to a reflective and contented mood. It prepares us for the next line and amplifies its meaning: 'All round the coast the languid air did swoon.'

Standing on the bluff of Sunderland's north eastern shore, as I did some years ago at St Peter's Church, Monkwearmouth, my imagined memories of our Saxon past were evoked by Bede's description of that same place where Benedict Biscop, the founder of the great Northumbrian monastery, lay dying. Bede wrote that the monks kept vigil in the church, reciting psalms throughout the hours of darkness as 'icy night rushed by in wintry gales'.

The North Sea and its wintry gales are never far from the story of our great Northumbrian saints. Benedict Biscop had once known a gentler climate. For some years, he had been a monk of Lérins, the island abbey off the Mediterranean coast of France. He would have felt the southern warmth of Provence and the languor of the long afternoons, aromatic with the scent of thyme and rosemary from the kitchen garden beyond the cloister. But his homeland drew him back to the north.

He knew that God was calling him to found a monastery there, and took home what he had learnt from the monastic communities on the Continent. He founded a monastery at Wearmouth (Sunderland) and later a twin community at Jarrow. Bede recalled that Biscop had done the following:

> *Crossed the sea so many times and never returned empty-handed or profitless, but brought back a goodly store of holy books… blessed relics of martyrs for Christ, masons to build the church, glaziers to decorate and also to secure the windows, then again he brought teachers for singing and for ordering the service in the church of the whole year.*

The manner of singing the liturgy – a basic element of the monastic life – was taught at Wearmouth by John, the arch-cantor of St Peter's in Rome. In Bede's words, it was Biscop's wish that John should instruct the monks 'the chant for the liturgical year as it was sung at St Peter's.' He taught them the 'theory and practice of singing and reading aloud'. These instructions were later recorded in writing and copies circulated to other religious houses in England.

Next in importance to singing the Office was the study and inscribing of sacred texts. We know from Bede's account of his own reading of the extensive range of Biscop's library. There is one remarkable survival from the scriptorium of his Northumbrian monastery: the *Codex Amiatinus*. It is a massive work, weighing 75 pounds and containing in a single volume almost the entire contents of St Jerome's Latin version of the Bible (the Vulgate). It is the earliest one still in existence, and is the only survivor of three versions made at the monastery of Wearmouth-Jarrow in AD 692. This volume, which was sent to Rome as a gift to Pope Gregory II, is testimony to the outstanding scribal skills of the Northumbrian monks, and to those acquisitive instincts that drove their founder first to track down, and then to acquire, one of the most valuable collections of classical and patristic texts at that time anywhere outside Rome.

St Peter's Church still stands on its windy headland at Monkwearmouth and so does her sister foundation, St Paul's, at Jarrow. Both churches contain fragments of Biscop's buildings, but of his great library, and collection of vestments, silks, tapestries, ivories and paintings, almost nothing escaped destruction by the Vikings. It is not so much the buildings that remain as the constant sea, with its windswept coast and the cry of the seabirds, that carries me back to those tough and weather-beaten monks gathered to recite the psalms as their abbot lay dying, and the icy night rushed by in wintry gales.

THE SCHOOL OUTFITTER

I was at Windsor looking for a hat. The Irish setter had taken a fancy to my ancient trilby and had eaten half the brim. By chance, I found myself outside the branch of my old school outfitters, Billings and Edmonds.

'A hat, sir? No, I am afraid we no longer sell gentlemen's hats.' It was a sad admission. 'There is not the demand,' he added, and, by way of explanation, he looked across at the only other customers. A mother and her eight-year-old daughter were in noisy debate over the regulation length of the school skirt. The child spoke bitterly and with great emphasis. The mother was close to tears. The middle-aged woman who was serving them tightened her grip on a large pair of tailor's scissors.

'Your London branch used to sell hats,' I said. 'In fact, I got my first one there. Must have been, oh, fifty years ago.'

'Would that be our shop in Prince's Street, sir?' he said, suddenly alert.

'The same,' I said.

He grasped my hand, speechless with emotion, and led me to the back of the shop. 'There,' he said, pointing to an Edwardian wall chart.

Beneath the firm's cartouche and date (1910) the chart displayed pictures of the clothing and accoutrements once considered essential to a young gentleman's wardrobe: silk top hat, felt hat, straw boater, tweed breeches, Eton collar, stockings, garters, woollen underwear and a variety of sportswear, including football jersey, tasselled cap and cricket flannels. All these were illustrated as worn by a twelve-year-old boy. In a corner of the picture, a small boy in a sailor suit, who might have been a younger brother, ran through a meadow with a butterfly net. It was a scene from Arcadia, but happily without the presence of Pan.

We stood in silence, deeply moved.

'Of course,' I said at last, clearing my throat, 'we no longer wore top hats and Eton collars.'

'Not even on Sunday?'

'Clothes rationing,' I said. 'It was 1946. Besides, Wellington House was considered to be a rather modern school.' I sensed his disappointment, and so I added, 'But St Peter's Court and Wellesley still wore tweed breeches in the winter term.'

'Ah, yes. St Peter's Court,' he murmured dreamily. We were now talking of a golden age. I felt that I had recovered some of my credibility. To confirm my position, I mentioned Hawtrey's. Although the school had left Westgate for Wiltshire long before my time, it was always a strong card to play.

I first visited Billings and Edmonds in Prince's Street (conveniently close to Hamley's) with my mother in 1946, when I was eight years old. It was an introduction to the big world I was about to enter, of Latin and French, cricket, chapel, showers, and dormitories. No young recruit could have been prouder of his new uniform and none more apprehensive. I was not the only one. There were other small boys and their harassed mothers, each clutching a long school list. To comfort us, there was kindly Mr Edmonds junior, known as 'Mr Denis', and his staff. There was also, in a glass cabinet, a large model of the recumbent Gulliver being tied down by tiny Lilliputians.

The official clothes list was largely unchanged from before the war, with the exception of tweed breeches. These had been replaced by navy-blue shorts, which we wore with grey woollen socks up to the knee. Garters were necessary. In design they were the same as those that had been worn with breeches. Unlike the rest of the population, who wore a simple band of elastic to keep their knee socks up, we used the traditional garter – a long, knitted band half an inch wide and about eighteen inches long. These we wound round the leg just below the knee, the fringed end being tucked in and pulled through, so that it showed below the top three inches of stocking, which we had folded down over the garter.

Occasionally, a boy would be spotted using elastic garters. 'That's no way for a gentleman to dress,' the headmaster would bark. 'Unhealthy too. Restricts the blood. Your toes'll drop off, and then you'll be sorry.'

The visit to the shop in Prince's Street in 1946 was the first of many. Five years later, when I moved on to my public school, I had to go to a large department store to be equipped. At the age of thirteen I learnt what it was to come down in the world. However, Billings and Edmonds had ways of retaining their old boys' loyalty. They engaged a senior cutter and a small team of seamstresses to supply the sartorial requirements of their teenage and adult clients. I still possess, and sometimes wear, the dinner jacket, overcoat and tweed suits they made for me over fifty years ago.

They were also remarkably indulgent. My headmaster, whose opinions on garters were forthright, had equally singular views upon the rest of his wardrobe. In the 1950s, Billings and Edmonds were still making for him Norfolk jackets and plus fours in thorn-proof tweed. They also created for him, to his own design, a hugely heavy blue serge jacket, which he called his harbourmaster's coat. It had double rows of crested brass buttons, removed from the livery of his former butler, and was built to keep out the bitter northeaster that on certain days howled through the school.

He regarded the school outfitter as his own personal tailor. In those days of proprietary schools, when headmasters ran their establishments as their own private households, the teaching and domestic staff occupied the same positions as had their predecessors in the larger country houses of the eighteenth century. The domestic chaplain, the family tutor, the music master, the lady-in-reduced-circumstances who gave drawing lessons, the housekeeper, the cook, the butler, the gardener, the groom, the boot boy, the peripatetic dancing master and the tailor, all had their modern counterparts in the private boarding school of the 1940s.

It was to this world that the school tailor would make his termly visit, with his tape measure, swatches and order book. Like the gardener who was required to coach cricket and the housekeeper who taught reading, the school tailor found himself having to put his skills to unexpected uses. One of his tasks had been to bind the handle of an old fives bat in the school colours of navy-blue and burgundy-red (the headmaster had been in the Coldstream Guards in World War I).

This ancient relic of an obscure variant of Rugby fives had been used to whack the boys by the formidable Victorian clergyman who had founded the school. It now hung on the wall in the dining hall, like Uncle Matthew's trenching tool in Nancy Mitford's *The Pursuit of Love*.

During our reverie before the Edwardian chart, we were both aware of the dismal sounds from the front of the shop. However, what until then had been a painful but muffled continuo now reached a sudden explosion of violence. Discussion, it seemed, had given way to physical conflict. The child, having been exasperated beyond endurance, had assaulted her mother and was now threatening the assistant with a lacrosse stick.

'Oh dear,' the manager sighed. 'I'm afraid you must excuse me.'

Tact required my rapid departure. I did not wish to witness the poor man's discomfiture. However, as I left the shop I saw him produce from beneath the counter a large jar of boiled sweets. He was evidently a man of infinite resource, well equipped to take Billings and Edmonds into the modern age.

THE RUSSIAN LADY

She sat in the shade of the veranda, bathing her hands in a bowl of scented water. This ceremony was repeated every morning, and, as a treat, I was sometimes invited to join her. I had to be quiet and not distract her with childish prattle. 'It is good to be silent, Ardrrianne', she used to say in her heavy Russian accent. 'Nyou must learren to be steell.' In her company, stillness was not hard to achieve, even for a fidgety seven-year-old. It was enough just to sit and stare in silent wonder. Sometimes she would turn and smile as she caught me watching her. When it was time for me to leave, she would ring for her *suffragi* (house servant) and ask him to bring us a dish of those exquisite marrons glacés from Groppi's, the famous Cairo confectioner and, surely, one of the wonders of the Levant.

The cool air of that veranda lingers in the memory; it was a delicious oasis in the burning heat of an Egyptian summer. And there were sounds too. I can recall the clink of her rings as she removed them one by one from her long fingers and placed them carefully beside her on the marble-topped table. One of them, a large sapphire, had belonged to her grandmother in St Petersburg. Sometimes she would tell me stories of her childhood in Russia before the Revolution, before she and her parents had fled and made their home in Cairo.

I can still hear, too, the soft ripple and splash as she moved her fingers to and fro through the water, and further away, the hiss and swoosh of the gardener's hose as he dampened the dust on the paths of the garden and its surrounding lawns, cool beneath the overhanging mango trees.

There was another, less welcome, noise: the mewing cry of the kites as they circled in the sky above us. That sound is always there, unbidden at the edge of my memory, signalling the menace of those ragged scavengers as they waited for their chance to swoop with frightening speed and accuracy, and seize a piece of carrion from the street, sometimes even snatching food from the hand of an unwary child.

People said that the kites once used to stay close to the smoking rubbish heaps and burial mounds of Fustat, the abandoned city of medieval Cairo. That was a long time ago. Since then, a new Cairo had sprung up the in the late 1860s when Ismail Pasha, the Khedive of Egypt, had ordered French and Italian architects to lay out a modern European city. The squares, tree-lined boulevards, palaces and pillared villas recalled the style of Baron Haussmann and earned the Egyptian city the name of 'Paris on the Nile'. It was here that the Empress Eugenie came, invited by the Khedive, to attend the premiere performance of Verdi's *Aida*.

Now the kites had found rich pickings among the careless Europeans in their garden suburbs of Zamalek and Maadi.

We were neighbours with the Russian lady and her English husband. Our houses were two of a pair, conjoined and built in the French style in Zamalek, a residential tree-lined quarter of Cairo. Other neighbours were British, French, Jewish, Armenian and Greek – a cosmopolitan population with a network of relations that spread across the Levant: Istanbul, Alexandria, Aleppo, Athens, Beirut, Smyrna.

By the time of my childhood, Cairo's *belle époque* was long since over, though there remained in the buildings, squares and tree-lined suburbs echoes of the Khedive's once graceful city. Among the expatriate residents – the old Levantine diaspora – there still lingered a few who remembered a golden past. Then, in 1952, came the revolution, followed in 1956 by the Suez débâcle, and it was all over. Cairo was reclaimed by its rightful owners, and we, the interlopers, packed our bags and left.

The Russian lady, by now a widow with a meagre pension, found refuge in London. My mother discovered her address from a mutual friend. The small flat in Earl's Court, over a dry cleaner's shop, was just within her means, though the stairs, she said, were difficult. However, the journey by bus to the Russian church in Ennismore Gardens was do-able, and she found a local delicatessen that sold *halawa* to remind her of Cairo.

The last time I saw her she was in a nursing home. She was propped up in bed, no longer able to speak, but still able to recognise me. I sat with her talking a little, but mostly silent and holding her hand. The sapphire ring now loose on her long bony finger had slipped round. When the time came to leave, I asked her if she would like me to say a prayer of blessing. She nodded and closed her eyes. Then, as I said the words, her right hand moved slowly to her forehead, down to her chest, then across to her right shoulder and then to her left in the Orthodox manner of signing the Cross.

I left the room quietly and closed the door.

TRAVEL BROADENS THE MIND

An Englishman's attitude to travel abroad is sometimes ambivalent. 'Don't go,' warned King George V, adding darkly, 'I know – I've been.' Uncle Matthew in Nancy Mitford's *The Pursuit of Love* believed that the only reason for going abroad was to fight the enemy. Otherwise, with such a beautiful country as ours, what was the point?

Against this advice, countless English people willingly and joyfully seize the earliest opportunity to travel overseas, and many return convinced that, though they do things differently abroad, they often do them better. That was certainly the opinion of Parson Yorick in 1768. 'They order, said I, this matter better in France', he wrote in the opening sentence of Laurence Sterne's *Sentimental Journey*, a novel that, according to the author, was meant to 'teach us to love the world and our fellow creatures'.

When Thomas Cook organised an eleven-mile railway excursion for members of his local Temperance Society in 1841, he had no idea what he was starting. By 1872, he was offering a two hundred and twelve day world tour for two hundred guineas. The journey included travel by steamship across the Atlantic, by stagecoach from the east to the west coast of America, by paddle steamer to Japan, and an overland journey across China and India.

How much easier travel abroad was once Mr Cook took us in hand and became our dragoman and our guide. Before he did so, travel abroad was a chancy business.

In the 1830s Alexander Kinglake made his famous journey through the Middle East to Constantinople, Jerusalem and Cairo. In his account (*Eothen*, 1844), he describes the *cordon sanitaire* that confronted English travellers as they left the safety of Christendom and entered the Ottoman Empire at Belgrade. Once across the Sava River, a tributary of the Danube, there was no return to Europe without a compulsory fourteen days' incarceration in the local lazaretto. Infection by the plague was a hazard of oriental travel, and anyone ignoring the quarantine laws was, in Kinglake's words, 'carefully shot and carelessly buried' outside the walls of Belgrade. This was evidently not a contingency covered by the kind of insurance we have since grown accustomed to acquiring before we set off on foreign travel.

Apart from being shot by border guards or infected by bubonic plague, the traveller in those days encountered other less serious risks. Tourists to the Holy Land expected to travel rough. William Thackeray's jaunt from *Cornhill to Grand Cairo* (1845) describes his arrival by steamer off the Palestinian coast at Jaffa, whence the tourists, both ladies and gentlemen, were carried through the surf on the shoulders of burly Arabs and deposited on the quay.

By the time Andalusia Riley and her husband, Athelstan, toured Europe in 1887, a railway network had been laid across most of the Continent, making it possible to set off from their house in Kensington in time to catch the morning boat train from Victoria Station to Dover, cross the Channel to Calais, and thence by train, with several changes, to Cologne, arriving at 11.30pm on the evening of the same day. She was a resilient traveller, but had to admit in her journal that at the end of the first day of their journey they were 'very hot, dirty, tired and awfully cross'.

From Cologne, they travelled for more than three weeks by train, riverboat and horse-drawn carriage, staying at Nuremberg, Vienna, Budapest, Sofia and Adrianople before eventually arriving at Constantinople. The last stages of their journey were by horse-drawn carriage, with their luggage following in a cart behind. The roads were dangerous and rough, the terrain wild, and the inns primitive. For their comfort, they stopped from time to time to brew tea at the roadside on their spirt lamp. For their safety, Athelstan wore his revolver, with a supply of cartridges to hand.

How different is our modern package holiday! It is now possible to spend a holiday abroad, say on the coast of the Red Sea, on a beach in Spain or on a cruise in the Aegean, and pass the entire ten days hearing nothing spoken but English. This is not what Sterne meant about learning to love the world and our fellow creatures. He was, after all, writing about the journey, not the destination.

Packing half a dozen shirts and a black pair of silk breeches, Yorick set off on an itinerary that was meant to take him through France and Italy. However, such were the delightful contingencies of travel – in his case the lady, the monk, the snuff box, the gloves, the passport, the *pâtisseur*, the sword, the letter, and, of course, that unexpected encounter with the *fille-de-chambre* – that he got no further than Lyon. He never reached Italy at all.

But what a journey it was – what a journey!

TIES WILL BE WORN

I was once asked to leave a smart London restaurant because I was improperly dressed: I was not wearing a tie. Well, that is not entirely true. I was not asked to leave *tout court*. I was given the option of putting on a tie, which the head waiter had most kindly provided. Evidently, he kept a supply for such an event. It was an uncomfortable experience, not least because at that time I was trying to impress my companion by my social poise and nonchalance. To be put down by a head waiter is a cruel but sometimes necessary experience for a young man who is putting on airs.

As the seventeenth-century statesman and essayist Francis Bacon might have said, 'Dress serves for delight, for ornament and for cover.' It also serves another purpose, as our forebears acknowledged when they drew up their sumptuary laws or, as we would say, their dress code.

Sumptuary laws regulated what citizens wore and, to a lesser extent, what they ate. In England, the first of these laws was introduced in 1363: the 'Statute concerning Diet and Apparel'. It was the first of seven similar dress codes that Parliament enacted over the next two hundred years. The preamble to the Act attacked 'the outrageous and excessive apparel of divers people against their estate and degree'. Exaggerated display of wealth was bound to lead, in the words of the Bill, to 'the great destruction and impoverishment of the land'.

The Act included a list of who might wear what. Knights were not permitted to wear ermine – that was reserved for a higher rank. Ploughmen and cowherds were to wear garments made from blanket and russet wool, costing no more than twelve pence apiece. The Act of 1463 was specific on the matter of pointed shoes – no one lower than a baron was permitted to wear 'pykes' (pointed toe pieces) longer than two inches.

There was nothing new in this attempt to control excess. In ancient Athens, as far back as the seventh century BC, no lady was allowed to be accompanied by more than one maid in public, unless drunk, in which case she could have two to support her. The concession, it was made clear, was for the woman's security, not for display.

The purpose of sumptuary legislation was not only to control excess but – and this was probably its chief aim – to make sure that people kept to their proper rank. To the medieval mind, the stability of society required a well-defined hierarchy. Everyone was to conduct himself or herself in a manner appropriate to his or her own station in life. You have only to read the prologue to Chaucer's *Canterbury Tales* to see how his characters are defined by their trade or profession and their dress. Chaucer tells us this:

Of each of them, so as it seemed to me
And which they weren and of what degree
And eek in what array that they were inne;
And at a Knight than wol I first bigynne.

There then follows that wonderful procession – yeoman, friar, lawyer, haberdasher, carpenter, doctor, miller, pardoner and so on.

Citizens were not trapped by these codes. Far from creating a caste system that inhibited social mobility, the sumptuary rules provided a ladder by which citizens might climb or descend. Look at the stories of Thomas à Becket, Dick Whittington, Thomas Wolsey, Thomas Cromwell and countless others who used the ladder to climb the ranks.

Distinction in dress was not simply a matter of ostentation, rather it was a question of civic propriety. Social stability required everyone to know his or her place, and to behave and dress accordingly. And nowhere were these distinctions more clearly on parade than at the weekly assembly every Sunday in church. The disposition of the pews in the parish church replicated the social structure of the community. The squire's pew was prominent in place and comfort. Other households had their family pews, each according to their social standing. Lastly the poor and the strangers were allocated their places on a plain bench.★

Today, we find such blatant distinctions – in church of all places – abhorrent. Does the Bible not have harsh words to say about making distinctions between rich and poor in the congregation (James 2:1–4)? The teaching in those verses is unequivocal. But the situation in England in the Tudor, Stuart and Hanoverian years was different from the early Church to which the Epistle of St James is addressed, and entirely different from the Church today.

In the days of, say, Queen Elizabeth 1, King Charles II or King George III, the congregation at prayer in church on Sunday was identical, in theory at least, to the population of the parish at home and at work on weekdays. It was the parish at prayer. The people did not come to church as individuals drawn away from their weekday world, in which case it would have been right for them to leave behind all secular distinctions of class and wealth. On the contrary, they came as the parish, a corporate body seeking to consecrate their local community, and because of that it was important to appear before God in their secular dress, as squire, farmer, artisan and labourer. To pretend otherwise would be to have missed the point of common prayer.

Today, we live in a different world. Our congregations can no longer pretend to be the local community at prayer. The sacred and the secular no longer overlap as once they very nearly did. We come now as individuals, called out of the world and leaving our secular roles behind. We come to build by God's grace the artificial, sacramental community of the Eucharist in which our worldly positions in society have no place. In that sense we come on Sunday to our worship no longer as the Church *of* England, but as the Church *in* England, and never has that little preposition made so big a difference.

Then, on Monday, we must return to our weekday world where distinctions of education, class, rank and wealth – our modern sumptuary codes – still have their part to play, and where it is always as well to check in advance whether 'Ties will be worn.'

* See *The History of Myddle* by Richard Gough (ed. David Hey, Penguin Books, 1983) for a contemporary account of a Shropshire village in the seventeenth century, based upon the allocation of pews in the parish church.

TURN DOWN AN EMPTY GLASS

Yon rising Moon that looks for us again –
How oft hereafter will she wax and wane;
How oft hereafter rising look for us
Through this same Garden – and for one in vain!

And when like her, O Sáki, you shall pass
Among the Guests Star-scatter'd on the Grass,
And in your joyous errand reach the spot
Where I made One – turn down an empty Glass!

Edward Fitzgerald (1809–1883)

Omar Khayyam (1048–1131)

Sáki, the servant girl, came barefoot across the lawn to the place where old Khayyam liked to talk. Oh, how he talked! On and on, sitting under a tree on silken cushions and sipping his wine. As she passed, he would take her hand and hold it for a while. But now all that was over. There only remained his empty glass. She bent down to take it, then changed her mind, turned it over and left it lying on the grass – a small gesture of farewell, unnoticed by the other guests who even then were calling for their glasses to be refilled.

Canon Claude Jenkins, last of the great Oxford bibliophiles and a noted ailurophobe, would always walk round, not over, Dr Pusey's ledger stone in the nave of Christ Church Cathedral. This small gesture of respect invariably caused a stumble in the procession, especially if there were any visiting clergy unprepared for the old canon's sudden shimmy to the right.

In Krakow, the Polish people honour the Jewish victims who died in the ghetto of their city during World War II. They have placed seventy empty bronze chairs around the city square, the Plac Bohaterow Getta, as silent witnesses to a dreadful crime.

At my school an empty desk once played its part. A week before the school reconvened after the Christmas holidays, we had heard of the death of one of our classmates. It had been reported in the national papers. He and his mother had been shot dead by his father, who had then turned the gun upon himself. For the first week of term his desk remained empty. Then a tactful rearrangement of furniture filled the gap. He had been fourteen years old.

An empty glass on the lawn, a ledger stone in a cathedral nave, unoccupied chairs in a town square, a vacant desk in a classroom. More than wistful sorrow, more than painful regret, more than the guilt of a monstrous crime, more, even, than the horror of violent murder, much, much more than all these cruel circumstances of dying is the mystery of death itself: The silent emptiness which replaces in an instant the presence of a living being.

SIDONIUS APOLLINARIS AND THE FALL OF ROME

Sidonius Apollinaris (AD 430–489) was a country gentleman who lived in fifth-century Gaul. He had held public office in the government at Rome, for which he was raised to the rank of patrician and senator, before changing careers and being appointed Bishop of Clermont.

When at home, he enjoyed a good read with his meal. He owned a well-stocked library and, after retirement from years of service to church and state, he found the leisure to read and write. His poetry, although technically accomplished, has been described as formal and lacking heart. He corresponded regularly with other members of the Gallo-Roman aristocracy who, he tells us, had been taught, like him, to think and write after the manner of Cicero and Virgil.

In a letter to a young friend in the year AD 470, Sidonius lamented the decline of Latin. He blamed the younger generation. Even if the language of civilisation survived, he said, its purity had been corroded by the 'rust of barbarisms' imported from the north. He did not underrate the ability of Theodoric, the leader of the Ostrogoths and later king of Italy, to assimilate southern culture. At Theodoric's banquets, Sidonius wrote, 'You can see the eloquence of Greece, the abundance of Gaul and the nimbleness of Italy'. Even so, there was a certain coarsening of style under the hybrid regime that then passed for imperial Rome.

Did no one tell them, these country gentlemen with their old-world manners, their books and their complaints about the post arriving late, that their civilisation had already ended? When, fifty years ago, Alaric's Visigoths had sacked the Eternal City and scattered the ashes of the Caesars across the pavements of imperial Rome, did no one tell them that AD 410 was the year when the light of civilisation had been at last put out? And, when they heard from correspondents across the Channel, writing from their country villas – some letters were still getting through – that the legions had long since marched away from Britain and taken ship, never to return again, did it not occur to them that everything had changed?

Of course they knew. They had long ago learnt to live in the ruins of empire. The signs of decay were all around and had been for years. Public buildings were neglected, communications failing, the people turning to strange gods, the military in mutiny and bureaucracy irretrievably clogged. The centre could no longer hold. And all the while barbarians from the north kept moving south and moving west, driven onwards by those behind, searching for pasture and sunshine.

Sidonius may have been overprotective of the ancient disciplines, but despite his nostalgia for the past he had found a pearl of greater price. In a poem, commissioned by the Bishop of Lyon and engraved upon the wall of a church in that city, Sidonius invited visitors, as they marvelled at the jewelled glory of the restored basilica, to sing their alleluias no longer to the old gods, but to the new one, Jesus of Nazareth.

'*Vicisti, Galilaee* – Thou hast conquered, O Galilaean,' sighed the Emperor Julian on his deathbed, while across his empire, on the walls and mosaics floors of countless rural villas, Christian symbols began to appear alongside images of Jupiter and Apollo*; on library shelves Virgil and Cicero now rubbed shoulders with the Early Fathers of the Christian Church.

The custodians of their ancient culture, the country gentlemen of Gaul, Britain, Spain and Italy, forsook their tired, old gods and found salvation in a new religion. In doing so, they christened the classics of ancient Greece and Rome.

There were others besides Sidonius who bridged the gap

between Virgil and Dante, and taught our forefathers how to build a European Christendom upon the foundations of a pagan culture. Prudentius, in fourth-century Spain, wrote hymns to the Holy Trinity in classical metres. Boethius, a senator in sixth-century Rome and close adviser to Theodoric, was the greatest classical scholar of his age. His *Consolation of Philosophy* was one of the works included by King Alfred as compulsory reading for the clergy, and his works on musical theory became standard texts at Europe's universities in the Middle Ages.

Europe's academe was shaped by the 'seven liberal arts' of antiquity: grammar, rhetoric, dialectic, music, arithmetic, geometry and astronomy. How pleased Sidonius Apollinaris and his correspondents would have been to know that soon (what's five hundred years in the span of history?) the classics that they had kept alive in their country villas, and which were then preserved by monks and nuns in their monastic libraries, would become the syllabus of the new universities at Bologna, Salamanca, Paris, Oxford and Cambridge.

---

* Excavations during the twentieth century at Lullingstone in Kent revealed a substantial Romano-British estate. Among the rooms of the villa was a chapel with murals showing the Christian Chi-Ro, and elsewhere in the building mosaics depicting Bellerophon riding the winged Pegasus and slaying the chimera.

JOHN DONNE

Poet and Priest (1572–1631)

(First published in the *Church Times*, March 2008)

John Donne, poet and priest, was raised a Roman Catholic due to his mother belonging to a recusant family and two of his uncles being Jesuit priests. After studying at Oxford and on the Continent, he was admitted to Lincoln's Inn. He won a reputation for brilliance among the circle of poets and wits of Elizabethan and Jacobean London. He bore arms under Essex and took part in the capture of Cadiz. For some years, he was secretary to the Lord Keeper, and a member first of Elizabeth I's and then James I's court. He was disappointed in his ambition to find preferment to public office. He was ordained at the age of forty-one. He was appointed rector of Sevenoaks, then reader at Lincoln's Inn, where he acquired a reputation as an outstanding preacher. In 1621, he became Dean of St Paul's, where he stayed until his death in 1631. The Church commemorates him on 31 March.

We know him first for his urgent lust, the tumbled sheets and naked mistress; all those brilliant verses of youth, incandescent and unashamed:

License my roving hands, and let them go
Before, behind, between, above, below.
O, my America, my new-found-land,
My kingdom, safeliest when with one man mann'd.

We know him last for his slow and public dying: the coffin placed in his bedroom at the deanery weeks before; the final portrait showing him wrapped in a funeral shroud, already purchased; his last sermon preached on Ash Wednesday 1631 before the court: '... those bodies that are the temples of the Holy Ghost [must] come to this dilapidation, to ruin, to rubbidge, to dust...' King Charles I, looking up at the preacher's emaciated face, thought that 'the doctor preached his own funeral sermon'.

Between those two – the young lover and the dying priest – came the courtier, the soldier, the poet, the Anglican apologist, the husband and father, the preacher and the friend. There was no sudden change of direction, no conversion on the road to Damascus, only a progression: from Rome to Canterbury, from frenzied liaisons to settled matrimony, and from court to church. Ordination was the result partly of persuasion by others (King James I, no fool in this case, saw in Donne priestly gifts) and partly because his career at court had foundered.

People spoke of his gentleness, and loved him. They remarked upon his musical voice. The king enjoyed his company at table, relished his wit and would ask him to read aloud.

Later, it was his sermons that so moved them; his poems, both sacred and profane, were not as widely known. Izaak Walton wrote about his preaching that it 'showed his own heart was possessed with those very thoughts and joys' that he spoke of. He was 'a preacher in earnest; weeping sometimes for his auditory, sometimes with them... and all this with a most particular grace and an unexpressible comeliness.'

There are, in his sermons, passages so densely crammed with scriptural texts and references to the Fathers as to be now unreadable. But there are others of such vivid intensity that they grab the mind. He preached to the court on 29th February 1628 that 'He that will die with Christ upon Good Friday, must hear his own bell toll all Lent.' And he went on to refer to the half-heard sound of the night watchman's bell, which lingers in the memory throughout the day beneath the cheerful noise of London's street musicians outside and the 'blessed music' of the choir of the Chapel Royal: 'It may be of use, that a poor bell-man waked you before, and though but by his noise, prepared you for their music.'

The melancholy note of the night watchman, like the tolling of the passing bell, resonates beneath the surface of his prose and poetry: 'Send not to ask for whom the bell tolls, it tolls for thee.' In his love poetry, there sounds a sadness beneath the frenzy. In his devotions, Donne prayed for release, to be brought 'at my last awakening into the house and gate of heaven, to enter into that gate and dwell in that house, where there shall be no darkness nor dazzling but one equal light, no noise nor silence but one equal music, no fears nor hopes but one equal possession, no ends nor beginnings but one equal eternity in the habitations of God's majesty and glory.'

METAPHOR AND RELIGION

'My love is like a red, red rose,' sang Robert Burns, and we all know what he meant. It is our habit to express our emotions in terms of physical phenomena. Love is a rose, courage is a lion, envy is green, fear holds us in its icy grip and patience sits upon a monument smiling at grief.

Our language and, to a certain extent, our thoughts, are constructed from and confined by the physical condition of our existence. We are compelled to speak of abstractions in material terms. We grasp an idea and weigh an argument. We see a difficulty and scent a danger. Mental process is described by touch, weight, sight and smell: metaphor is the default position of almost all our conversation and philosophy.

Then why – you might wonder – do people who are so accustomed to this well-used and necessary device in their daily lives suddenly become stubbornly literal in their understanding (or, one might say, wilful misunderstanding) of the language of religion?

So much time has been wasted and ill-feeling generated by the debate about the creation stories in the first chapters of the book of Genesis. Read as a literal description of the beginning of time they never made much sense, but read as they were intended to be read, as poems of wonder, and as prayerful meditations on the glory of a coherent universe experienced as it is now and not as it might have been in the distant past, they are as true today as they were when first composed.

There is nothing at all incompatible between the Darwinian theory of evolution and the ancient song of creation (Genesis 1:1–2:3). They both engage with the physical universe, but in different ways. One is a scientific theory, and uses observation and analysis to account for the different forms of life and how they came to be the way they are. The other is a poem, and uses the metaphor of a seven-day narrative to celebrate the wonder of creation. One is about method, answering the question 'How?' The other is about value, provoking the exclamation 'Wow'. Both share the belief that the universe is a complex but coherent unity to which we belong in fellowship with all other living species.

Here is another beautiful metaphor for creation:

The sun is but a little spark of God's infinite love. The sea is but one drop of his goodness. But what flames of love ought that spark to kindle in your soul; what seas of affection ought to flow for that drop in your bosom.

Thomas Traherne (1663–1674)

FRANCIS WRANGHAM

Godliness and Good Learning

Francis Wrangham was a Yorkshire parson with a large library. In his time (1769–1842), his views on Catholic Emancipation were perceived as dangerously liberal and ensured that he remained unmitred. He was, however, an archdeacon, and, as such, his reputation for efficiency and scholarship led Dr Edward Venables Vernon Harcourt, Archbishop of York, to describe him as 'an ornament to my diocese'. Sydney Smith, another Yorkshire parson and a great diner-out, thereafter referred to his friend as 'Ornament Wrangham'.

Wrangham, like many of his generation, was well read in the classics, and wrote translations of Horace and Virgil. He made translations, too, from French and Italian works, and his correspondents included Wordsworth, Byron and Walter Scott. He was a bibliophile and collector of rare books. His library was so extensive – over fifteen thousand volumes and one thousand bound collections of tracts – that he was compelled to build an extra wing to his vicarage in Hunmanby. After his death, his books were shipped from Filey in two barges to London, where they were auctioned at Sotheby's, with the sale taking twenty days to complete.

But he was no mere ornament. His pastoral concern for his flock led him to set up a dispensary for the sick, a savings bank, a village cow club (a co-operative society to assist parishioners in the loss of the family cow) and a parish library. Of the parish library, which was housed in the vestry, he wrote the following:

> *The schoolmaster attends on Sundays for half an hour prior*
> *to the beginning of the morning service to receive and give out*
> *books as are returned or required, and 15 or 20 volumes are*
> *usually exchanged upon these occasions.*

He seasoned his piety and charitable works with humour. On doing duty at a neighbouring church and being warned before the service that a turkey was nesting in the pulpit, he advised the congregation that in those circumstances he would not preach a sermon, which, anyway, he was sure would not be missed.

Many years after his death, one of his daughters wrote to her children:

> *None of you can remember his charming manners, the*
> *sweetness and tenderness of his smile, the elegance of his*
> *language, the suavity of his reproofs, so that the servants used*
> *to say they liked being found fault with by master – he always*
> *seemed so to have trusted them and been fond of them.*

JOSEPHINE BUTLER

Social Reformer (1828–1906)

(First published in the *Church Times*, May 2011)

Josephine Butler (née Grey) was born into a well-to-do family, in which Whig politics were undergirded by evangelical piety. A cousin was Lord Grey who, as prime minister, had piloted the 1832 Reform Bill through Parliament. Josephine married an Anglican clergyman, George Butler, who supported her in her campaigns for social and educational reform. Her crusade on behalf of the victims of child and adult prostitution in Britain, on the Continent and in India, laid the foundation of a new attitude to women's rights and child protection. The Church commemorates her on 30th May, which was the day of her death in 1906.

'Beautiful and histrionic, meticulously dressed and coiffed, Butler was adored by men and women alike' begins her entry in the *Dictionary of National Biography*. But, from an early age, she had been haunted by the accounts she read of poverty and injustice.

A happy marriage, and the birth and upbringing of four children occupied her for many years, until the accidental death of one of her children changed the course of her life. Her little girl, in a moment of high spirits, had tripped and tumbled from the first-floor landing to the floor below. The distraught mother wrote the following:

> *Never can I lose that memory. The fall, the sudden cry and then the silence... I became possessed with an irresistible desire to go forth, and find some pain keener than my own.*

In 1864, her husband was appointed headmaster of Liverpool College. Josephine began to visit the women's vagrant ward of the Brownlow Workhouse, where she joined the inmates in picking oakum. She spoke to them about the saving love of Christ and taught them to pray. Later, she described the 'great sigh or murmur of vague desire and hope, issuing from the heart of despair, piercing the gloom and murky atmosphere of that vaulted room, and reaching the heart of God.'

Her extraordinary strength of purpose, and undoubted powers of rhetoric and drama found their outlet in a national campaign to repeal the Contagious Diseases Acts of the 1860s. This legislation was designed to control the spread of venereal diseases in garrison towns by submitting prostitutes to compulsory medical examination. A specially recruited police force was given powers to arrest on sight any woman who was, or might seem to be, a prostitute. This led to cases of brutality, corruption and injustice.

In the course of one year's campaigning, Josephine Butler travelled two thousand seven hundred miles, addressing ninety-nine meetings and four major conferences. She became the target of violent abuse and social ostracism. *The Times* described the campaign as a 'hysterical crusade' led by 'prurient and cynical fanatics'. The Annual Church Congress in 1872 greeted George Butler's speech on the subject with an angry howl, to which he replied that if the clergy failed to take up the cause, the country would turn against the Church of England with the cry, 'Away with it! Why cumbers it the ground?'

The Contagious Diseases Acts were repealed in 1886. However, there was an even greater evil to which she had by now turned her attention. Child prostitution was protected by Parliament's reluctance to raise the age of consent from twelve years to sixteen. A bill to this effect had been thrown out by the Commons in 1883. It was only when the journalist,

William Thomas Stead, published his account of a ruse by which he persuaded a reformed brothel-keeper to purchase for £5 a twelve-year-old girl from her parents for the purpose of prostitution – a 'sting' in which Josephine Butler herself was reluctantly complicit – that Parliament rushed through an Act raising the age of consent to sixteen years. The threat of exposure by the press had put both Houses in a panic.

Josephine travelled to many of the major cities on the Continent to observe and campaign. In Belgium, she was instrumental in the arrest of the chief of police for his part in trafficking women between Brussels and London. In Paris, she harangued the prefect of morals, M. Lecour. He was later sacked by the French government, but rewarded by his friends for his services to the women of France with the post of honorary bell-ringer of Notre Dame.

'Economics lie at the root of practical morality', Josephine wrote. Poverty was what drove women into vice, not *la coquetterie*, as Lecour had insisted, while dismissing the problem with a Gallic shrug. Education, training and employment must be the remedy. She published over ninety books and pamphlets on women's education. 'The closing off of occupations to women precipitates poor women downwards into prostitution.'

What sustained her? Her lifelong habit of prayer. She said, 'All prayer resolves itself into communion... Face to face with Jesus, all perplexities vanish.'

CATHEDRAL CHORISTERS

(Sermon preached in Guildford Cathedral
at Evensong on 15th January 1989)

Earlier in this service, a new chorister was admitted to the choir. He is the latest in a succession of boys to take his place in the choir of Guildford Cathedral. Since the consecration of this cathedral twenty-eight years ago about one hundred and twenty boys have been choristers. On average, each of them has spent, or will spend, four of his most impressionable years singing the weekday and Sunday services. At an average of fifteen hours singing a week (seven hours in services and eight in practice), and, allowing for holidays, a chorister can reckon to spend six hundred and fifteen hours a year singing. And those of you who are good at mental arithmetic will already have calculated that six hundred and fifteen hours represents eighty-eight working days, taking a working day of seven hours' duration.

Now, you might wonder, those of you who have sons in the choir, what effect all this will have upon the growing boy. Well, it is not the purpose of this sermon to propound theories about the spiritual, physical, mental or social effects that sustained choral exercise may have upon your sons, considerable as those effects undoubtedly are.

Nor is the purpose of this sermon to tell you what you already know or what you will soon find out: that the day you surrender your son to the choir is the day you surrender yourselves and your other children to four years of the cathedral treadmill.

You choir parents are, however, a resilient lot, especially

the mothers. You must not think that the dean and chapter are unaware of the sacrifice, in terms of your time and domestic dislocation, that having a son in the choir entails. We are enormously grateful for your heroic support.

I thought it might be useful this evening to set your sons into the long perspective of history. And it is a long perspective. The cathedral tradition, to which your sons now belong, goes back a long way into the medieval history of Europe. Guildford Cathedral is modern – only twenty-eight years old – but its constitution and its purpose are set deliberately within the tradition of the greatest medieval cathedrals of Europe.

To understand that tradition, you have to realise that the cathedral is a collegiate foundation. It is a college of canons, lay clerks and choristers, whose role is to perform the daily routine of worship. This routine continues throughout the week and throughout the year. It is not merely a Sunday routine. It does not derive its validity from the number of people sitting in the nave. The worship is equally valid whether there are two hundred and fifty people present, as there were at the Sung Eucharist this morning, or whether there are two people present, as there may be at Evensong tomorrow.

That, I think, is the essential thing you must grasp about your sons' work in the choir. They are not singing for the benefit of an audience, but to the glory of God.

I was talking to someone the other day about our weekday Evensong and explaining that there are occasions (particularly Monday evenings in the winter) when there is no one present in the nave at all. 'Well, then,' she said, 'what is the point in having a service when there is no congregation?' But who said anything about there being no congregation? The choir of a cathedral is the congregation; it is the regular worshipping community, the college, that meets daily and that is joined on Sundays by an extended congregation in the nave.

That is the theory that underlies the existence of a cathedral. The building serves many other purposes, but they are secondary to its chief function, which is the daily performance of choral worship.

Mind you, theory and practice do not always match. During the long history of cathedrals and collegiate churches, there have been times when choirs have fallen on bad times; times when the behaviour of the choir and the clergy has fallen far below any recognisable standard of reverence.

It used to be the custom during the nineteenth century for the choir at Westminster Abbey to wander individually into their stalls before the service. As they arrived, they would greet each other casually and sometimes noisily, and they would continue in private conversation until the striking of a clock signalled that the service had begun. It was just as well that the sparse congregation was given this signal, for otherwise it was not apparent from the conduct of the choir that worship had started.

The choristers of York Minster in the eighteenth century were so badly behaved that, after one particularly disgraceful outbreak of rowdiness, the precentor felt it necessary to imprison the ringleaders in the dean and chapter gaol.

The conduct of the lay clerks was even worse – if that were possible. The precentor of Durham Cathedral, J B Dykes, found that the only way he could persuade the men of the choir to attend a practice was to call upon them individually in their lodgings and to beg their attendance as a personal favour. Mind you, cathedral lay clerks could not be blamed entirely for their conduct. So poorly were they treated by the clergy, so low had they sunk in their self-esteem, that they inhabited an underworld populated by out-of-work music-hall performers and seedy musicians, reduced to scraping an uncertain living by giving piano lessons to maiden ladies, and singing glees at gentlemen's dining clubs. Inevitably, they found solace in the bottle.

Nor were the clergy always much better. In the 1840s, one of the canons of Rochester, partially paralysed as a consequence of apoplexy, brought on by a surfeit of beef and claret, had to be carried to his stall for the Daily Office by his butler and the head verger. It was hardly a dignified way to start Evensong.

Now all that has changed. A brief acquaintance with Guildford Cathedral Choir will convince you that we have all come a long way since those bad old days, clergy, lay clerks, choral scholars and choristers alike. The theory of worship and its practice have moved closer together. Of course, in different ways, we still fall short of the ideal.

Take, for example, our wandering thoughts; those irritating distractions that disturb your mind during the service. When you sit there in the nave on a weekday evening listening to the magnificent music, and hearing the incomparable language of the Bible and the psalms, you should, of course, be rapt in devotion. You would like to be. But, more often than not, you are busy calculating exactly how little time Psalm 78 is going to leave you to get your son back home for his homework, to get your daughter off to her ballet class and to collect your husband from the station.

If you feel like that, and it would be unusual if you didn't occasionally, then you can imagine how clergy and choir members are likewise distracted by the mundane vexations of daily life.

We all fall short of the ideal. But the ideal is still there, to be reached for, though never grasped. And we the clergy, the gentlemen of the choir, your sons and yourselves are all party to this daily endeavour to perform the perfect act of worship in honour of Almighty God.

LITTLE GIDDING

(From an article published in the *Church Times*,
December 2006)

It was far from any thoroughfare – a decayed manor house close to a ruined church – but it would suit their purpose. When old Mrs Ferrar saw the nave of the little church full of hay, and the windows broken, she led her family in the work of restoring and furnishing it. 'In those additions of structure and ornament that have been made to the material of our church', wrote her granddaughter Anna, 'there was none of our family that had not a share.'

Mrs Ferrar's son, Nicholas, was the inspiration and leader of the community at Little Gidding. He had long felt the call to a life of prayer. Trinity Sunday in 1626 was his appointed time. He rose before the house had awoken, and walked along empty streets from the City, down the Strand and past the village of Charing Cross to Westminster Abbey. There he was privately ordained deacon in King Henry VII's chapel by William Laud. 'Believe me,' Ferrar's former tutor told Laud, 'You have never ordained such a man and probably never will again.'

'Since the great things of the earth vanish', Ferrar wrote to his cousin, 'let us set our designs and desires where they cannot fail... let us begin to live.' At the age of thirty-four, after a full and successful career in the world, he withdrew from society to begin to live.

In time, the word got out. People came across the fields to visit. Some out of curiosity. Some to ridicule. Some 'to kneel where prayer had been valid'*. Bishops, poets, priests, and men and women from all walks of life. King Charles I came twice: the first time in majesty and the second 'by night as a broken king'. No visitor was turned away and none was treated with special favour.

What they saw was a family household of thirty to forty members, ranging in age from Mrs Ferrar's seventy years to the infancy of the newborn grandchild, bound together in a routine of prayer, study, work, singing and recreation.

A surgery and dispensary were opened at the house for the neighbourhood. A large dovecote was converted into a school. Sixty gallons of gruel was prepared weekly for the poor. Broth was distributed to the sick.

This was not a religious community in the usual sense. It was not a society of like-minded adults drawn together by a common purpose. This was a family of parents, children, brothers, sisters and cousins. After his death, the community continued for some years until dispersed by the Civil War. In 1646, the church was ransacked and partially destroyed by Cromwell's soldiers. It was rebuilt in the next century and has been twice restored. Of the manor house, no trace remains. There the story began and there it ended: a disclosure of grace suspended in time.

* *Little Gidding* by T S Eliot.

THE CORN WAS ORIENT AND IMMORTAL WHEAT

(First published in the *Church Times*, 8th October 2004)

The streets were paved with golden stones,
The boys and girls were mine;
Oh, how did all their lovely faces shine!
The sons of men were holy ones,
Joy, beauty, welfare did appear to me,
And everything which here I found,
While like an angel I did see,
Adorned the ground.

From 'Wonder' by Thomas Traherne (1637–1674)

For Thomas Traherne, the material world was translucent with the glory of its creator: 'Eternity was manifest in the light of the day, and something infinite behind everything appeared.' He never lost that intensity of vision by which, as an infant on the brink of childhood, he experienced a timeless world:

> *The corn was orient and immortal wheat, which never should*
> *be reaped, nor was ever sown… and boys and girls tumbling*
> *in the street, and playing, were moving jewels. I knew not*
> *that they were born or should die.*

Little is certain about his life, and he would have remained unknown to posterity were it not for the chance discovery, in 1896, of a manuscript volume of his work on a second-hand book barrow in the Farringdon Road. Further manuscripts of his verse and prose turned up over the next seventy years, the latest being in 1967 when a volume was salvaged from a rubbish tip in South Lancashire.

In maturity, he learnt to incorporate his child-like vision within the forms of Anglican devotion. Religion did not sour his joy. The universe was 'no foul and pestilent congregation of vapours', as it so often appeared to the Puritan mind. Life was a glorious scene illuminated by men and women, no less than by God's holy angels. But it required a Christ-like vision to see the world transfigured thus in glory:

> *Your enjoyment of the world is never right, till every morning you awake in Heaven; see yourself in your Father's palace; and look upon the skies and the earth and the air as celestial joys.*

His *Centuries of Meditations* must be appreciated not simply as beautiful writing, but as part of a routine of prayer, sacrament and pastoral work. A friend wrote that Traherne:

> *Was much in love with the beautiful order and primitive devotions of this our excellent church, insomuch that I believe he never failed any one day either publicly or in his private closet to make use of her public offices, as one part of his devotion.*

Traherne's words were golden, but, like George Herbert's, they would have remained mere words were they not grounded in prayer and good works.

As an infant, he inhabited a world in which everything around him was glorious in its timeless present, having no past or future. As an adult, conscious of time, he welcomed the Church's restored calendar: it imposed upon the drift of days a divine chronology. The festivals and saints' days were 'the ornaments of time… the days of heaven seen upon Earth, the seasons of melody… the lucid intervals of the year.'

He never lost his sense of belonging to the human race. For him, devotion was not a solitary indulgence:

We infinitely wrong ourselves by laziness and confinement…
all creatures in all nations and tongues and peoples praise
God infinitely… You are never what you ought till you go
out of yourself and walk among them.

As a child, he had been thrilled by the sight of an empty banqueting hall filling up with 'lords and ladies and music and dancing'. The empty hall had been transformed by people. '[Then] I perceived that men and women are, when well understood, a principal part of our true felicity.'

This sense of community was given liturgical expression by the newly restored *Book of Common Prayer*. Its emphasis upon *common* worship, its provision of prayers for 'all sorts and conditions of men' and its occasions of special intercession, such as Rogation Days, taught him 'to be affected with the great and public concernments of the nation and kingdom in which we live, espousing the benefit and welfare of all.' 'Soften our king's heart,' he prayed, 'and teach our senators wisdom.'

He was gregarious by nature. In a notebook of private thoughts he wrote 'Thou, Lord, hast made thy servant a sociable creature for the praise of thy name; a lover of company; a delighter in equals; replenish the inclination which thyself hast implanted.' But, at times, he felt the need to curb that inclination:

Profound inspection, reservation and silence are my desires.
O that I could attain them. Too much openness and proneness
to speak are my disease… Speaking too much and too long
in the best things.

He chose a simple life. He died, as he had lived for some years, a member of the Bridgman household at Teddington. Among his few bequests were a ring to Lady Bridgman, the widow of his late employer, and sums of money to the servants of her household. He left to his brother his books and his best hat. But unmentioned in his will is his greatest legacy to posterity: the verse and prose meditations of a Christian in love with God and his creation.

THE TILLING BOURNE

The Tilling Bourne (or Tillingbourne) rises on Leith Hill and passes through the Surrey villages of Wotton, Friday Street, Abinger Hammer, Gomshall, Shere, Albury and Chilworth before joining the Wey near Shalford. If English history is shaped by our great rivers, such as the Thames, the Tyne, the Trent and the Avon, then this is surely no less true of the influence both in peace and war of this delightful little Surrey stream.

In its brief course of barely eleven miles, the Tilling Bourne and the country it passes through reflect the violence of our history as well as its peace. For several centuries its waters drove the mills for the manufacture of gunpowder. The mills were established at Wotton and Abinger by George Evelyn under licence from Queen Elizabeth I in 1589, and later from King James I. According to the agreement, two thirds of their output was supplied to the royal arsenal at the Tower of London.

George Evelyn's grandson, the diarist John, benefitting from a fortune derived from the fuel of war, devoted his life to the gentler arts of peace. He became a founder member of the Royal Society, and a leading expert on garden design and trees. He drew up a scheme for cleansing the polluted air of London, to which end he introduced the planting of plane trees in St James's Park. As commissioner for improving the streets of London, he ordered the paving of the quagmire he called *Pigudillo* (Piccadilly). During the turbulence of the Civil War, he sought temporary refuge in the family home at Wotton, where he made for himself a fishpond and 'a little study over a cascade, to pass my melancholy hours, shaded there with trees.'

After a life of public service, Evelyn retired permanently

to the family estate at Wotton, where he wrote of the Tilling Bourne:

> *I do not remember to have seen such variety of mills and works upon so narrow a brook, and in so little a compass; there being mills for corn, cloth, brass, iron and powder.*

Further down the stream, at Chilworth, gunpowder mills were established by the East India Company in 1626 under licence from King Charles I. During the Civil War the mills supplied gunpowder to the Parliamentarian army. They continued to be used up to end of World War I and were finally closed in 1920.

Chilworth still shows evidence of its explosive past. Longfrey, a fine five-gabled, three-storey house, now in private ownership, was originally built in the nineteenth century as separate dwellings for the mill foreman, and three workers and their families. In the valley there remain the ruins of the former gunpowder mills and associated buildings, as well as the protective mounds and bunkers.

During their three centuries of production, the Chilworth powder mills, with up to six hundred employees, were the scene of a number of catastrophic accidents and loss of life. In 1760, an explosion was violent enough to smash the walls of St Martha's Church on the hill above the village, leaving it in ruins until it was rebuilt in 1850.

Since the closure of the mills in 1920, the site has been allowed to return to nature. A survey in 2006 by the Surrey Wildlife Trust discovered the presence of a number of rare and endangered species enjoying the isolation and cover of more than eighty years of unhindered growth of vegetation, among them a family of dormice. Chilworth is a designated conservation area, managed by Chilworth Conservation Ltd and dependent on volunteers.

The past five hundred years of English history have seen immense changes to our landscape, with these changes reflecting not least the alternating demands of war and peace. The gentle Tilling Bourne, as it flows from Leith Hill towards Guildford through eleven miles of Surrey countryside, bears witness to those changes no less eloquently than all the great rivers of our land.

THE NUNS OF BARKING

They say that in Saxon times the nuns of Barking wrote passable Latin verse. We should not be surprised. After all, study of the classics survived the fall of Rome and continued to illuminate what we used to call – but now know better – the Dark Ages.

In the seventh century Aldhelm, Abbot of Malmesbury, composed Latin verse and wrote authoritatively about classical prosody. Later, Bede wrote his *History of the English Church and People* in Latin, which was the only language common to a readership that extended throughout Britain and the continent of Europe. Bede wrote one life of Cuthbert in hexameters and another in prose.

In eighth-century York, where the Minster library contained not only the works of the Early Fathers, but also those of Pliny, Virgil and Cicero, Alcuin's reputation as a classical scholar was so great that Charlemagne headhunted him and persuaded the Yorkshire scholar to join the royal court at Aachen as tutor to the royal princes and schoolmaster to the empire.

Thus, the influence of Latin endured, not only as an instrument of government, but as the language of theology, philosophy, liturgy, poetry and love.

In the tenth century the works of classical authors were part of a student's syllabus. Priests in their colleges and nuns in their cloisters read the plays of Terence to sharpen their conversational Latin and polish their literary exercises. '*Humani nil a me alienum puto*' ('I count nothing human as foreign to me'), they quoted to each other, and felt the pleasurable frisson of classical humanism.

The tenth-century German nun, Hroswitha (Roswitha) a canoness of Gandersheim, herself a poet, admitted to being somewhat troubled by her enjoyment of the plays of Terence. In the preface to her own plays she wrote the following:

> There are many (and we cannot entirely acquit ourselves of the charge) who are attracted by the polished elegance of the style of pagan writers and prefer their works to the holy scriptures.

In the twelfth century, Aelred, abbot of the Cistercian community at Rievaulx, wrote that his favourite reading as a schoolboy in Durham had been Cicero's treatise on friendship, *De Amicitia*. He based his own treatise *De Spirituali Amicitia* on the work of Cicero. Like the nuns of Barking, he found space for a gentler humanity in the harsh world of the cloister.

'Those who take friendship out of life, take the sun out of the world,' he wrote, and it was noted how he had brought to that bleak abbey on the North Yorkshire moors the comforting warmth of southern sunshine.

CONTINUITY OF THE CHURCH

Thomas Ken (1637–1711)

(First published in the *Church Times*, June 2000)

When Thomas Ken first went to Winchester College in 1651, the boys still doffed their hats to the statue of Our Lady as she looked down from her niche above the gate. William of Wykeham's collegiate foundation carried into the seventeenth century an unbroken continuity with its pre-Reformation past, as did those other corporate bodies that then constituted the Church of England: the clergy, the cathedrals, the parish churches and the universities.

To understand Ken, one must see him and the Church of England within that continuity. He wrote the following in his will:

> *I die in the Holy Catholic and Apostolic Faith, professed by the whole church, before the disunion of East and West; more particularly I die in the Communion of the Church of England as it stands distinguished from all papal and puritan innovations, and as it adheres to the doctrine of the Cross.*

He sealed his will with a signet ring engraved with the figure of our Lord crucified upon an anchor. The ring had once belonged to John Donne, who had given it to Izaak Walton, Ken's guardian and brother-in-law. It had then passed to Ken.

Although barely a century after the Elizabethan Settlement, Thomas Ken's ministry, first as a priest and then as a bishop, nurtured the growth of an already established lay spirituality rooted in the *Prayer Book*, as had George Herbert's a generation earlier. At his first parish at Little Easton near Dunmow in Essex parishioners, including his patron's wife, Lady Maynard, would join him in church on weekdays for the Daily Office.

In one of his poems he describes the qualities of a parish priest:

Give me the priest these graces shall possess –
Of an ambassador the just address:
A father's tenderness, a shepherd's care,
A leader's courage, which the Cross can bear…

He had courage and did not hesitate to rebuke vice. When Charles II required Ken's prebendal house in Winchester to accommodate the royal mistress, his billeting officer met with a stern rebuff. The king was impressed and did not forget. He appointed to the next available see, Bath and Wells, 'the little fellow who refused poor Nelly a lodging.'

One of Ken's appointments was that of chaplain to a naval expedition to the British base at Tangier. He went at the king's command, accompanying Pepys on board *HMS Grafton*, one of a small fleet whose orders were to blow up the harbour and evacuate the British colony. When they arrived, they found the expatriate community demoralised, the admiral drunk and the governor debauched. But, on this occasion, as Pepys recorded, Ken's attempt boldly to rebuke vice failed to have any effect.

His refusal to comply with James II's arbitrary and unconstitutional Declaration of Indulgence was inspired not by a desire to disoblige the English Roman Catholics, whose interests the king hoped to promote, but by a wish to keep himself and the clergy of his diocese within the law. It was this act of defiance, shared by the Archbishop of Canterbury and five other diocesans, and their brief incarceration in the

Tower of London, that precipitated James's flight into exile and hastened the establishment of a constitutional monarchy.

To many Thomas Ken's subsequent refusal to swear the oath of allegiance to James's successor, because to do so would be in breach of his existing oath, appeared quixotic. To Archbishop Sancroft, Bishop Ken, six other bishops and four hundred clergy, all of whom faced deprivation rather than take the oath, it was a matter of conscience.

After a long retirement, spent mostly as private chaplain to Lord Weymouth at Longleat, he died in 1711. In the evening hymn that he had written for the boys of Winchester occur these words:

> *Teach me to live, that I may dread*
> *The grave as little as my bed;*
> *Teach me to die, that so I may*
> *Rise glorious at the aweful day.*

For many years it had been the custom of this ascetic and most devoted servant to rise each morning long before the sun and late at night to lie down to sleep wrapped in his own funeral shroud, so that when his Lord came he would be ready.

THE LANGUAGE OF MUSIC

Thomas Tallis

(From a sermon first preached in York Minster at
Evensong on Whit Sunday, 1985, in the fourth centenary
year of the death of the composer Thomas Tallis)

We ought to thank God this Whit Sunday, not only for his inestimable gift to us of music but also for the very survival of Church music in our time. That we have been able to hear tonight an anthem by Thomas Tallis – indeed, that the Church is able to continue to praise God through the medium of this kind of choral music at all – is nothing short of miraculous, when one considers the obstacles it has had to surmount in the past.

Chief among these obstacles has been an exaggerated belief in the power of words alone to express the mysteries of our faith and to convey the riches of the Gospel. Theologians are compelled to reduce religious experience to the limited scale of words. That is their job, and we must not blame them if in doing so they lose some of the vitality and exuberance of faith.

But if it is the function of theology to diminish truth to the dimension of words, it is certainly not the job of liturgy so to do. The function of liturgy is to release us from the tyranny of prose by allowing us to respond to the Holy Spirit of God in choral and instrumental music, in the movement of ritual, in the music of words, in the soaring beauty of architecture, in the colours of textiles, and in the graceful shapes of visual design.

When Thomas Tallis composed this evening's anthem, *If ye love me, keep my commandments*, the future of Church music was under threat from many of the reforming clergy. Clergy were trained (as they still are) theologically. They were also trained (as they still are) to instruct. Not surprisingly, they had then (as they still have) a bias towards verbosity. It is not that they use too many words, but that they attach too much importance to the words they use.

Thomas Tallis and his contemporaries four hundred years ago were attacked by some of the more vocal clergy because, it was claimed, their music distracted the worshippers' attention from what the clergy believed was the essential part of worship: the words.

English Church music suffered much at the hands of the reformers. Archbishop Holgate, in his visitation to this Minster in the year 1552, ordered that only the plainest of plainsong must be used; the music to contain, as he put it, 'no reports and repeatings'. The organ was to be locked up. The vicars choral, song men and choristers were to apply themselves to something useful, like learning the New Testament by heart.

They had been taught to regard the Church as a big-bosomed mother, ample in her proportions and generous in disposition, but now they were confronted in her place by the prim aspect of a niggling governess. It was all so dismal: the nagging verbosity of Protestantism. Happily, theological fashion changed. Two years later the organ was unlocked, the music restored and the archbishop sacked.

Even so, the general climate of ecclesiastical opinion was so repressive that musicians such as Tallis, Byrd and, later, Gibbons and Purcell, established the English choral tradition in spite of, rather than because of, the clergy. However, experience teaches us that, when a movement continues to flourish in spite of clerical opposition, it is often the work of the Holy Spirit, and that explains why our cathedrals four centuries after the death of Thomas Tallis are musically in better health than they have ever been.

Praise the Lord in the sound of the trumpet; praise him upon the lute and harp.
Praise him in the cymbals and dances: praise him upon the strings and pipe.
Praise him upon the well-tuned cymbals: praise him upon the loud cymbals:
Let everything that hath breath: praise the Lord.

Psalm 150:3–6

PLAIN ENGLISH

One of the foundation texts of our language, the 1611 King James Version of the Bible, is written in the plainest English. Just how plain is sometimes not recognised.

Most of us encounter the Bible in the formality of a church service. The public occasion lends a solemnity to the sentences when they are declaimed from the lectern. Should we read our own copy at home, as likely as not, its sombre leather binding and its print in double columns of small font have an oppressive effect. We do not expect to be startled. We do not expect to be amused.

But if we read those sentences from a paperback version, say, of St Mark's Gospel, while seated at the kitchen table or standing by the stove, book in hand, waiting for the potatoes to boil, or on a Kindle in a railway train travelling through the English countryside – in short, if we detach our minds from all the weighty associations of a sacred text – those same sentences will leap off the page with the fresh vigour of direct speech. We can hear Jesus himself as he talks to his critics in the temple at Jerusalem or to the crowd in Galilee. Not even the old diction of 'thee' and 'thou', or 'hast' and 'hath', can obscure the vitality of his words.

Take three familiar passages from the King James Version:

He that is without sin among you, let him first cast a stone at her.

John 8:7

Consider the lilies of the field, how they grow; they toil not, neither do they spin.

Matthew 6:28

A sower went out to sow his seed, and as he sowed, some fell by the wayside.

Luke 8:5

What you notice about those sentences is the simplicity of their construction and their use of short monosyllabic words. It is their child-like clarity that has endured for four hundred years with the need for barely any alteration to make them intelligible to us in the twenty-first century. They do not sound in the least bit archaic. If you use a good modern translation, such as the New Revised Standard Version, you will be surprised how few changes were necessary. It preserves the character as well as much of the text of the King James Version.

The reason for this simplicity is that William Tyndale, upon whose version of 1525 the King James Version of 1611 and all later ones have been based, translated the New Testament from the original Greek in which it had been written, and not from the Latin version (the Vulgate) that had been commonly used throughout the Middle Ages.

The use of the original Greek text had a profound effect, not only upon the accuracy of the translation but upon the style and cadence of the English in which it was written. Tyndale himself explained the difference between a translation made from the Latin and one from the Greek:

For the Greek tongue agreeth more with the English than with the Latin. And the properties of the Hebrew [of the Old Testament] agreeth a thousand times more with the English than with the Latin.

With the Greek text, he said, all you need is to translate it word for word and in the same natural order of common speech, but to translate the Latin, 'Thou must seek a compass.'

Another foundation text of our language is Bunyan's *Pilgrim's Progress*, which was written about sixty years later than the publication of the King James Version of the Bible, but derived from it the same simplicity and clarity of diction. As an example, this well-known passage written in direct and unadorned language shows the power of plain English:

> *When the day that he must go hence was come, many accompanied him to the river-side, into which as he went, he said, "Death, where is thy sting?" And as he went down deeper, he said, "Grave, where is thy victory?" So he passed over, and all the trumpets sounded for him on the other side.*

The effect of such a simple style is profound, but it masks its achievement. To write simple English is not easy. For various reasons, writers who want to make an impression find it easier to write in an ornamented style. The result can be splendid, allusive and wonderful in its elaboration. Through it, the author shows off his skill and flatters the reader, but the style itself comes between the subject and the reader.

Compare Bunyan's words or the Gospel narrative with the consciously literary style of Thomas Browne, the Norwich physician and polymath who was Bunyan's contemporary. He opened his great *apologia* for the Christian faith, *Religio Medici,* with the following baroque sentence:

> *For my Religion, though there be several circumstances that might persuade the world I have none at all, as the general scandal of my profession, the natural course of my studies,*

the indifference of my behaviour, and discourse in matters of Religion, neither violently defending one, nor with that common ardour and contention opposing another; yet in despite hereof I dare, without usurpation, assume the honourable style of a Christian.

Wonderful stuff and I love it! In those rolling, Latinate constructions, we hear the voice of Thomas Browne, a most singular and erudite old gentleman. But in the Gospel narrative, where we encounter someone for whom only plain English will do, we hear the voice of Jesus.

BEWARE FALLING ROCKS

(A sermon preached in York Minster at the Sung Eucharist
on the first Sunday of Lent, 1985)

Dust thou art and unto dust shalt thou return.

Genesis 3:19

I am sure that you will agree that, whatever else we might say about the state of our roads, we cannot complain that we have not been warned. There is no shortage of admonitions. Along the margins of the carriageway stand countless signs telling us of the hazards that lie ahead: sharp bends, narrow bridges, T junctions, falling trees, leaping deer and many other such contingencies. And necessary they are too, these highway caveats, for we have become accustomed to their presence and have learnt to rely upon their help.

But what are we to make of a wholly different category of roadside warning? A category only rarely encountered, but nonetheless disturbing. 'Beware Low-Flying Aircraft' is an admonishment that appears to invite no appropriate response, save, perhaps, a cautious removal of one's hat. 'Road Subject to Subsidence' contains enough menace to upset one's peace of mind, without offering any evidence on which to base an alternative plan of action. Likewise, the doom-laden warning 'Falling Rocks'; to this apocalyptic threat there is no answer.

It is, of course, no new thing, this appetite we have for frightening ourselves silly with imaginary disasters. Heaven knows, the real disasters are bad enough without adding to them the menace of what horrors might, just might, lie round the next bend in the road.

There is a strong temptation to introduce into our religion what might be called a 'high scare factor'. Indeed, for some people, the very purpose of religion is to scare us out of wits; to stampede the sheep as they safely graze; or to panic the sons of Belial. You might think that that is precisely what this season of Lent is all about: that it is a time for being shocked into repentance. 'Dust thou art and unto dust shalt thou return'; these words echo in the memory like a tocsin as we are carried on our rattling tumbril down the avenue of years to our appointed end.

But no, that is not the purpose of Lent. It is not the purpose of our Christian faith to threaten and dismay us with rumours of disaster. It is not the duty of the preacher to create panic in his hearers.

Charles Spurgeon, the popular Baptist preacher in the nineteenth century, was a great orator. At the height of his career, he preached weekly to a congregation of several thousand in the Metropolitan Tabernacle in London. Being an old-fashioned Calvinist, his sermons were full of hell, fire and indignation. The people loved to hear themselves castigated for the sins of the world. The more violent the rhetoric, the more they liked it. 'Ye worthless atoms of existence, ephemera of the day,' he declaimed, 'Ye creeping insects on the bay-leaf of time!'

It was strong stuff. But whether it did more than just create a pleasurable frisson of fear in his fashionable audience is another matter. I would say that to be reminded that one is no more than a 'creeping insect on the bay-leaf of time' is to be exposed to the same high scare factor as when one is told that the stretch of road ahead might, just might, at any moment open up and swallow us as it did the unfortunate Dathan and Abiram★. These warnings might turn out to be true, but they serve no good purpose, for there is nothing we can do to avert the disasters they predict.

If it is not the purpose of the Christian religion to frighten us out of our wits, then what, you might ask, is its purpose?

This brings us back to the text I began with: 'Dust thou art and unto dust shalt thou return.' The words come from the book of Genesis. They are part of the story about Adam. There are, in fact, two stories about the creation of Adam: in the first, God creates him by divine *fiat*, that is to say, by the divine command 'Let us make man in our own image.' In this story, divine utterance was the agent of creation. In the second story, God is a craftsman moulding Adam from the earth, breathing life into his nostrils. Far from being a metaphor for destruction, dust is the material of God's love.

Lent is a time to reflect upon God's loving purpose for each one of us, by which our Creator, if we allow him, cleanses and fashions the base material of our daily lives into the glorious body of his Son, the second Adam, who is the image of the invisible God and the firstborn of all creation.

* Psalm 106:17

SEATING ARRANGEMENT

(A sermon preached in Guildford Cathedral at the Sung Eucharist
on the seventeenth Sunday after Trinity, 1989)

*When thou art bidden of any man to a wedding, sit not down
in the chief seat, lest a more honourable man than thou be
bidden of him; and he that bade thee and him come and say
to thee, 'Give this man place', and thou begin with shame to
take the lowest seat.*

Luke 14:8–9

'Do come in,' you are told as you nervously face the
interviewing panel. 'Do come in. Take a seat.' The offer is polite
and graciously implies that there are several seats from which
to choose. There is only one; a hard and uncompromising
little piece of furniture, placed on its own in the middle of
the room before a row of interrogators. And so you sit down,
isolated, exposed and in mortal dread.

There is, of course, the other kind of interview, more
usual these days, when the seat you are offered is not
isolated, but part of a cosy circle. Instead of being hard and
unyielding, it swallows you up in its voluptuous embrace.
Someone I know, rather short in stature, so seriously
misjudged the depth of the seat she was offered – more a
sofa than a chair – that she spent the first five minutes of
the interview struggling to get her feet back to the floor.
It was not easy from that supine position to convince her
interviewers, who loomed above, that she was the hard-
nosed director of finance they were looking for.

Seats, chairs, ottomans, thrones, benches, misericords and pews – so many different designs, but with one single function: something to be sat upon. And yet they can serve a secondary purpose. Now, you would think that the universal need to take the weight off one's feet would make the chair a symbol of shared humanity. But it is not so. The chair can be a symbol of status or of rank, rather than equality. Not that such distinctions are always unwelcome. After all, life would become inexorably dull, and not one whit more just, if there were no high table at which one might be invited to sit, no Treasury bench in the House of Commons, no Woolsack in the House of Lords and, bearing in mind where we are this morning, no bishop's throne in Guildford Cathedral.

The point that Jesus was making was not that status in itself is wrong, but that the pursuit of it is. The delusion of grandeur, which promotion sometimes brings, can make us look unconscionably silly. Maybe we need to be reminded that, whatever level of status we achieve in our careers, it is all part of an elaborate game. Once we take it seriously, things get nasty.

Luckily, it is impossible to take rank seriously. Perhaps the titles that often go with promotion are deliberately absurd as a warning; for example, Gold Stick in Waiting or Master of the Rolls. Maybe that is why clergy acquire such strange titles. There is a heavy irony in ascribing to a priest the title 'Reverend' which, after all, means 'he or she who must be revered'. The irony deepens as a cleric ascends the professional ladder. Deans are addressed formally as 'Very Reverend', though never to their face. Bishops are addressed as 'Right Reverend'. Archbishops are addressed as 'Most Reverend'. As for archdeacons, well, it was suggested that they be called 'Hardly Reverend', but that seemed unkind, and so they are formally addressed as 'Venerable'. And you may make of that what you will.

But let us return to our seats.

There is one particular seat in a cathedral that causes embarrassment to its occupant: the bishop's throne. Here in Guildford the bishop's throne is a fairly modest affair compared with some of the grandiose structures in other cathedrals. But even on its reduced scale it sends out the wrong message.

In the early Church, the clergy sat in a semi-circular apse at the east end of the cathedral. In the centre sat their bishop. His position relative to his clergy expressed the ancient doctrine that episcopal authority derived from the corporate body of the Church, and so the bishop sat within that body. Later, when the bishop's authority was thought to derive by divine mandate directly from above, and his chair had become a throne, it was necessary to move it to a position over against instead of alongside his clergy. He was no longer the chairman, but the autocrat of his diocese and 'monarch of all he surveyed'.

It is this monarchical aspect of episcopacy, which is visible in the isolation and splendour of the bishop's throne in our cathedrals, that is now so misleading. It is fair to say that it no longer represents the beliefs or practice of today's bishops.

Finally, there is one aspect of a chair, whether it is that of a university professor, a magistrate's bench or a bishop's throne, that is obvious: a person who sits down cannot draw a sword (just you try, and see what happens!). Enthronement, even of a monarch, implies government by consent, not force.

SODA WATER BOTTLES

(A sermon preached in Guildford Cathedral at the
Sung Eucharist on Trinity I, 1988)

*If they hear not Moses and the prophets, neither will they be
persuaded though one rose from the dead.*

Luke 16:31

Dives, the rich man, made the same mistake as we all make. He thought that his wayward brothers would be converted by something miraculous. If only someone were to rise from the dead and confront them, then they would turn away from folly and wickedness. But he was mistaken – and so are we – in thinking that a supernatural intervention is likely to be more persuasive than the evidence of our daily lives.

Jesus himself was reluctant to use miracles to compel belief. He rebuked those who asked for supernatural signs and, when he did exert his divine power to heal or exorcise, he was at pains to do so with as little display as possible.

There remains within us all a desire for the supernatural and miraculous. But, annoyingly, our lives remain stubbornly earthbound, humdrum, commonplace and even *banal*.

'Oh, for a little bit of divine intervention,' we sigh, 'fire and brimstone perhaps (so long as it does not hit me), a vision, a visit from the Archangel Gabriel, or a martyrdom to encourage the faithful.' Now martyrdom – *there's* something we don't see much of these days in the Church of England. As Charles Gore said to William Temple, 'In the Early Church you had Holy Communion at supper, and after supper you proceeded to martyrdom. If only we proceeded to martyrdom after supper, we could do anything.'

Well, we don't do martyrdom here. Nor, on the whole, do we hear voices or see visons. As for the Archangel Gabriel, he has not been seen in Surrey for years. And so, like it or not, we must find our faith and practise our religion on a terrestrial level of existence, in the unremarkable circumstances of ordinary life, and without the benefit of signs and wonders.

James Tissot, the French painter who enjoyed great success in the 1880s, was rather grandly dismissed by Oscar Wilde for depicting ordinary people and ordinary things: 'He paints overdressed, common-looking people and ugly, painfully accurate representations of soda water bottles.'

Well, I don't know about you, but I rather like Tissot's paintings. Wilde may have been right in describing their subjects as common, but he was wrong to claim that only the extraordinary and beautiful are worthy of attention. One of the artist's roles is to consecrate the ordinary and to ennoble the commonplace. Think of Van Gogh's kitchen chair.

Now, is that not also the function of our religion: to consecrate the ordinary so that even the commonplace reflects the glory of the Creator? When God became incarnate in Palestine, he consecrated all humanity. The whole human race, that great mass of ordinariness, now bears the image of divinity. When he took bread, gave thanks and broke it, he consecrated the commonplace to bear the imprint of his grace.

To find God, we do not need to cross the seas, penetrate the clouds or climb the Alps. We need look no further than here; we need wait no longer than now.

THIS ENGLAND

'Patriotism is the last refuge of a scoundrel,' said Dr Johnson, and yet no one loved his own country more than he. We must take it, then, that the Great Cham was speaking of the xenophobic bigotry that gives patriotism a bad name. Love of one's country is surely love of one's home writ large, and who is to blame us for that?

Patriotism – at least, the English variety – was born in the sixteenth century, for it was then that there entered our ancestors' minds the *idea* of England. In 1544, John Leland wrote to King Henry VIII:

> *I have so travelled in your dominions both by the sea coasts and the middle parts, sparing neither labour nor costs, by the space of these six years past, that there is almost neither cape, nor bay, haven, creek or pier, river or confluence of rivers, breaches, washes, lakes, meres, fenny waters, mountains, valleys, moors, heaths, forests, woods, cities, burghs, castles, principle manor places, monasteries, and colleges, but I have seen them; and noticed in so doing a whole world of things very memorable.*

John Leland and his successor William Camden gave us a new perception of our country. Thanks to the map-drawing skills of Christopher Saxton and, later, John Speed, we began to know the shape of England and her counties. In Shakespeare's words, it was now possible to see our country as:

> *This other Eden, demi-paradise,*
> *This fortress built by Nature for herself*

Against infection and the hand of war,
This happy breed of men, this little world,
This precious stone set in the silver sea

Camden's *Britannia* revealed, for the first time, a land in which the destiny of her people was shaped by her landscape: her maritime coast with its profusion of estuaries, inlets and harbours; her great rivers and little streams; the contours of her hills and valleys; her mountains and dales; her high moors and rolling plains; and her woods, meadows and pastures: all so much more than just our habitat. These were and are our nursery, our school, our workshop, our playground, our home and, at the end, our final resting place where our mortal remains will lie commingled with the soil.

A new patriotism was possible. We were now able to picture our country as a precious stone set in a silver sea. We could now imagine, even though we might never visit, its entire coastline. The old loyalty, which had been born of fealty to the king, was now replaced by one which sprung from love of our country.

Our ancestors, who four hundred years ago began to know their Bible, saw England in biblical terms as a land flowing with milk and honey, with every man sitting beneath his own vine and under his own fig tree. Its rivers, too, entered the language of our poets. Edmund Spenser called the Thames as witness in his celebration of a marriage:

Sweet Thames, run softly till I end my song.

For Milton, the Severn became 'Sabrina Fair':

Sabrina Fair,
Listen where thou art sitting
Under the glassy, cool, translucent wave,

In twisted braids of lilies knitting
The loose train of thy amber-dropping hair:
Listen for dear honour's sake,
Goddess of the silver lake;
Listen, and save.

It was a land of flowers too, listed by a new generation of botanists and herbalists. Shakespeare would have known the work of his contemporary, John Tradescant the elder, and may have had in mind the Warwickshire countryside when he wrote Oberon's lines in *A Midsummer Night's Dream*:

I know a bank where the wild thyme blows,
Where oxlips and the nodding violet grows,
Quite over-canopied with luscious woodbine,
With sweet musk-roses and with eglantine:
There sleeps Titania sometime of the night,
Lulled in these flowers with dances and delight

But a Bible-reading people could not forget their patriotic obligation to protect society's casualties, the widows and orphans, and 'the stranger within their gates'. They heard read in church on Sunday how the ancient Hebrews had been immigrants in their Promised Land as all of us in England are and always have been. There cannot be a single one of us whose earliest forefathers were not born abroad and were not once strangers in this land we now call ours.

It is the landscape that makes us English, more so than our descent, more even than our language, race or creed. The land that Leland surveyed and Saxton mapped was here before our ancestors arrived and will still be here to shape the lives of others long after we have gone. They will come first as strangers as we did once. Then, striking inland and settling, they will find a deep delight in this island with her rivers and valleys, her meadows and flowers, a land that was given to us and that we must not deny to them.

And when they hear, as they most surely will, a single blackbird singing on a summer evening, feel the wet sand beneath their feet as they tread the shore at low tide, hear the wind blowing through the trees, smell the wet earth after rain, walk an ancient downland path, take the ferry cross the Mersey, or stand at the break of day with Wordsworth on Westminster Bridge and see the flowing Thames and London 'wearing like a garment the beauty of the morning', then will they be as English as the land they live in; then, like us, they will love the country that they have learnt to call their own.

ACKNOWLEDGEMENTS

The author wishes to thank the editors of the *Church Times* and *Save Our Parsonages* for permission to reprint articles which originally appeared in their journals, and Messrs Faber and Faber for permission to print extracts from *Sunday Morning* by Wallace Stevens.

ALSO BY ADRIAN LEAK

Nebuchadnezzar's Marmalade Pot

Brief, sharp, witty and profound – these reflections are in the best pastoral tradition of the Church of England – they make us chuckle, help us think and show us a glimpse of 'heaven in ordinary'.

Angela Tilby, Canon Emeritus of Christ Church, Oxford

It was George Herbert who noted that the good country parson is 'a diligent observer and tracker of God's ways', setting up 'as many encouragements to goodness' as possible. There could not be a better description of Adrian Leak who, in this wise and accessible collection of reflections, holds a compass that guides us through both the Church's year and the seasons of the heart. Celebrating the richness of the ordinary, he helps us appreciate that, at the end of the day, Christians are called to nurture the human capacity to look and to love.

Mark Oakley, Canon Chancellor of St Paul's Cathedral, London

Adrian Leak's brilliantly observed reflections make a fascinating read. They will appeal not only to Anglicans, including lapsed ones, but also to the large number of people who, while they have not been blessed with the gift of faith, care deeply for the Church of England. Adrian draws his inspiration initially from apparently superficial incidents and details, but as he gets drawn in he plumbs the depths and writes most movingly about the spiritual life and the problems of pursuing it in a largely indifferent and often hostile world. He claims his reflections are merely random meditations, but in fact they display the workings of a profound and mature intelligence.

Roger Lockyer, Reader Emeritus in History
in the University of London